A Complete Missions Awareness Program

A SUNDAY FOR THE WORLD!

"LET THE PEOPLES PRAISE THEE, O GOD;

LET ALL THE PEOPLES PRAISE THEE.

LET THE NATIONS BE GLAD

AND SING FOR JOY."

—PSALM 67:3,4

BILL STEARNS
World Christian, Inc.

Gospel Light

PUBLISHING STAFF
William T. Greig, Publisher
Dr. Elmer L. Towns, Senior Consulting Publisher
Dr. Gary S. Greig, Senior Consulting Editor
Jean Daly, Managing Editor
Pam Weston, Editorial Assistant
Kyle Duncan, Associate Publisher
Bayard Taylor, M.Div., Editor, Theological and Biblical Issues
Debi Thayer, Designer

ISBN 0-8307-1824-9
© 1996, William Stearns
All rights reserved.
Printed in U.S.A.

HOW TO MAKE CLEAN COPIES FROM THIS BOOK

YOU MAY MAKE COPIES OF PORTIONS OF THIS BOOK WITH A CLEAN CONSCIENCE IF:

- you (or someone in your organization) are the original purchaser;
- you are using the copies you make for a noncommercial purpose (such as teaching or promoting your ministry) within your church or organization;
- you follow the instructions provided in this book.

HOWEVER, IT IS ILLEGAL FOR YOU TO MAKE COPIES IF:

- you are using the material to promote, advertise or sell a product or service other than for ministry fund-raising;
- you are using the material in or on a product for sale;
- you or your organization are **not** the original purchaser of this book.

> Note: This one-Sunday program can be customized to fit the needs of your own church, campus fellowship, organization, denomination or affiliation of churches. You can:
>
> - Add your group's name at the top of each participant's sheet before photocopying.
> - Add you own key prayer requests on the Family Activity Guide and the Prayer Guide by simply covering over the printed prayer points before photocopying.
> - Even without altering the text or layouts in the program, feel free to improvise, stretch over several days, add more events or reduce the number of activities in your program. *A Sunday for the World* is for your group to celebrate God's heart for every people.

DEDICATION

To Amy, beloved coworker in encouraging the church to a vision beyond itself.

ACKNOWLEDGMENTS

Special thanks for many of the concepts, not only in this resource, but also in the overall current mission movement, go to Ralph and Robert Winter, Steve Hawthorne, Bob Blincoe, Bob Sjogren, Todd Johnson, David Barrett, Patrick Johnstone, Dave Bryant, Don Richardson, Kaleb Jensen, Jan Bell, Sandy Koop, Kathy Felty and the creative staff of the Caleb Project.

CONTENTS

OVERVIEW

INTRODUCTION

As we're following Jesus, we tend to watch very carefully for our own personal next step: Where is He leading me next? Am I growing properly as a Christian?

But Jesus often shook up His disciples' preoccupation with their own steps. His command in John 4:35 is startling: "Lift up your eyes!" As anyone who's grown up on a farm knows, it's reasonable to watch your step when walking through a field, but it's also stultifying if that's the range of our vision. "Look on the fields!" (John 4:35).

We're walking through the middle of a wonderful, terrifying, exciting, challenging global harvest field ripe with diverse cultures. And that broad perspective is crucial to see how our walk with Him fits in with His great, worldwide plan.

A global perspective of God's heart for every people is also important to see how our local church ministries can be infused with a vision beyond ourselves.

Especially in the Western church, we believers need to get better at lifting up our eyes. If we interpret our discipleship in Jesus Christ only in light of what we see in our own backyards, we're going to miss the historic miracles sparkling around us as He continues to make disciples of every nation.

May we not keep looking at our feet and miss the beauty of the whole Body, fitted and joined together and building itself up in love—from Novosibirsk to New Jersey.

THE EMPHASIS

The material of *A Sunday for the World* is from a solid biblical perspective as well as a realistic worldview that acknowledges the plight of the world's lost, the poor, the lonely and oppressed. Too often believers miss the balanced concept of the Two-Handed Gospel—offering the hope of salvation through the blood of Jesus Christ in one hand while with the other hand meeting physical and social needs in Jesus' name.

A Sunday for the World is not an opportunity to point long, judgmental fingers against believers for their lack of compassion for the world. It is not about pleas for finances. It's not a tirade against the apathy of Christians or the affluence of Western Christians. It really is a positive, surprising celebration of what God is doing in our world today.

Getting in on what God is doing in the big picture is presented in realistic ways. That is, everyone regardless of age or ministry focus can respond. This is not a recruitment blitz for new missionaries (although some prospects may surface from this celebration). This is not one of those fine programs to which most believers must yawn, "I guess this

WHAT IS THIS?

- *A Sunday for the World* gives your fellowship a new vision of God's heart for the world. It is a packet of one-Sunday activities for every age group in your church.
- It provides:
  —Promotional materials and ideas;
  —Bible lessons for each age group;
  —A whole-church Sunday service;
  —Special follow-up activities for small groups, families, prayer warriors and shut-ins.

EVERYTHING YOU NEED IS ENCLOSED

With a jump-start from *A Sunday for the World*, your fellowship can move into more informed, strategic action to turn your world upside down for the cause of Christ.

Overview

(See Outcomes.)

isn't for me." You can expect ripples of enthusiasm from across the fellowship: "God is doing some wonderful things in our world. I'd like to get in on this." (See Outcomes.)

THE PRESENTATIONS

As you noticed on the Contents page, there's quite a bit going on during *A Sunday for the World*, but it all centers around the Sunday Service presentation. For a focused summary of the overall program, review the Sunday Service.

What's the Theme of All of This?

A Sunday for the World doesn't really follow a traditional missions theme. You'll notice we don't use the *m* word in any of the presentations. In our culture today, that word *missions* conjures up in too many minds something far-off, odd, old, guilt-inducing, not-for-me, money-focused and smacking of a tiny agenda of a tiny interest group of fanatics. So we don't harp on missions—even though you're probably using this program on a Missions Sunday. So don't call it a Missions Sunday; simply call it *A Sunday for the World*!

The Theme Is:

* God loves every ethnic group on the face of the earth (see the 2s & 3s Bible Lesson, for example);
* So He blesses us as His people to bless every people—our own included (see the Junior High Bible Lesson, for example);
* So each of us has a specific role in some phase of that plan (see the Leadership Session about infusing all the church's ministries with a single vision—from ministries within the church to those that bless our own culture to those focused on blessing the nations);
* And we can rejoice together about the progress we see in God's global plan—a plan that will culminate some day in a streets-of-gold celebration we'll enjoy with every people, tribe, tongue and nation (see the message of the Sunday Service, for example).

OUTCOMES

At the close of your *A Sunday for the World* activities:

* Expect from 10 to 20 percent of your adults to indicate interest in a follow-up Bible study on God's global plan.

This outcome can be anticipated by offering a *Catch the Vision 2000* or the video-based *Destination 2000* course at the next available quarter of Bible study. These Bible studies are available through your local Christian bookstore or by calling 800-MISSION. (See Action Steps.)

* Expect perhaps 3 percent of your congregation—children included—to indicate interest in pursuing cross-cultural ministry.

Nearly 80 percent of missionaries say they sensed God's leading to missions between the ages of 10 and 12, so plan to conserve those indications of interest even among the children. (See Resources for children, youth and adult mission materials.)

WHAT COMES AFTER A SUNDAY FOR THE WORLD?

What comes next is up to you. A natural step would be more global and biblical education and training. Then comes action.

STUDY

You can provide this next-step education during your normal Bible study periods. Recommended adult Bible studies include:

* *Destination 2000* video course;
* *Catch the Vision 2000* Bible study.

(See Resources for more information on these plus youth and children's studies. See also Action Steps.)

ACTION

Following this solid Bible study input, many in your fellowship will want to get together regularly for some form of a mission fellowship—not to do the business of missions that demands a missions committee but to fellowship around global-scale news, prayer challenges and ongoing education. You can expect this core group then to initiate the kind of training programs, short-term opportunities and long-term involvement to move your fellowship from global awareness to strategic global impact.

- Expect about a dozen questions to be posed to your church leadership.

These include everything from "I don't believe these reports!" to "How many of our missionaries are working among unreached peoples?" to "What do we do and where can we get more information?"

This outcome can be facilitated by assigning a computer wizard with a modem to tap into Genesys, the global computer network with information and contacts throughout the worldwide Body of Christ. For a free sample session, your computer whiz can call 703-750-0318. He or she can share this key information with your entire fellowship. (See Action Steps.)

- Expect a surge in prayer power. Perhaps 50 percent of the Sunday Service congregation will indicate a commitment to fresh prayer.

The Service Notes sheet distributed during the Sunday Service allows participants to indicate their desire to pray for the world during the week. The Family Activity Guide encourages whole families to enjoy prayer activities together. The Prayer Guide, usable by any youth or adult, is especially designed to encourage shut-ins to realize their key role in God's global prayer strategies. (Resources to facilitate ongoing prayer interest are suggested under Resources.)

In the meantime...

"Look among the nations! Observe!
Be astonished! Wonder!
Because I am doing something in your days—
You would not believe if you were told."
Habakkuk 1:5

HOW TO HOST A SUNDAY FOR THE WORLD

(Check ❑ when completed.)

AS SOON AS POSSIBLE

❑   With your mission and Christian education committees, set the date for *A Sunday for the World* and mark your church calendar.

TWO TO THREE MONTHS BEFORE YOUR SUNDAY FOR THE WORLD

❑ 1. Decide what you want to do.

As presented, the components of *A Sunday for the World* simply fill in the programming slots most churches already have on a week-to-week basis: Sunday School sessions, a Sunday service, perhaps small study groups.

Still, you can simplify even more by choosing from the list below the combination of components that best meets the needs and schedule of your congregation. Or develop your own plan to use *A Sunday for the World* to begin or climax a mission conference, to train a mission-minded core group in a retreat setting or special seminar, etc.

A Sunday for the World Major Components

> ~ *Leadership Session—As a preliminary meeting, an at-home fellowship, a retreat, etc.*
>
> • Commentary • Take-Home Thought-Provoker

The enclosed Leadership Session gears the leaders of your fellowship to think through the integration of local and global vision. Leaders are to read through the commentary before gathering. The Leadership Sessions ideally should occur well before the *Sunday for the World* program, but even scheduling it after the special Sunday will enhance your leadership's outlook on how God may be leading you into more strategic involvement in His global plan.

> ~ *Bible Lessons—During Sunday School, children's church, mid-week Bible study classes, etc.*
>
> • Teacher's Commentary and Lesson Plan • Age-graded Worksheet • Family Activity Guide

The enclosed reproducible lessons for Sunday School, children's church or other Bible study meetings are designed to include all age groups in your *Sunday for the World* emphasis. Simply distribute the appropriate sheets to the teachers. No special meeting or preparations other than those listed on the teachers' guides are necessary. Each teacher simply follows the step-by-step instructions.

> ~ *Sunday Service—During a morning or evening service*
>
> • Message • Service Notes sheet

A Sunday for the World message outline is provided. Some prior coordination of the events of the service, of course, is suggested. (See planning item number 4 below.) Still, other than typical preparation for worship and musical presentations, the service actually requires little prep time.

The enclosed reproducible Service Notes sheet—to be inserted in the bulletin or handed out for the sermon—has a tear-off section to record responses to the message.

> *~ Follow-up Activities—During the following week*
> • Small Group Study Guide • Family Activity Guide • Prayer Guide

The enclosed reproducible Small Group Study Guide is designed to follow up your *Sunday for the World* message. The guide directs groups to study more of the biblical principles of God's global plan. No supervision or special preparations other than those listed on the guide are necessary; even if you have no regular small group program, ad hoc groups will enjoy an exciting study as they follow the simple step-by-step instructions.

The reproducible Family Activity Guide provides two family sessions to reinforce the message during the week. The Prayer Guide is especially for those not able to attend the service, assuring them of their crucial role in God's global plans. Of course, it can be used by anyone wanting to pray.

No supervision or direction is needed for the Family Activity Guide or Prayer Guide.

❏ 2. Determine which committee members will be responsible for:
- Photocopying materials;
- Implementing promotion;
- Facilitating the Leadership Session (if part of your emphasis);
- Distributing Bible Lessons to age-group teachers (if part of your emphasis);
- Distributing Study Guides to small groups (if part of your emphasis);
- Facilitating the events of the Sunday Service;
- Handling any necessary equipment setup and operation;
- Compiling follow-up responses.

❏ 3. Indicate the number of photocopies of the enclosed materials your *Sunday for the World* will require.

We will need:

_____ copies of Promotional Poster 1

_____ copies of Promotional Poster 2

_____ copies of Promotional Leaflets sheet

_____ copies of the Leadership Session Commentary

_____ copies of the Take-Home Thought-Provoker (one per participant)

(Consider photocopying children's Sunday School worksheets on brightly colored paper.)

_____ copies of the Nursery Worker's Information Sheet

_____ copies of the Bible Lesson for 2s & 3s (Teacher's Guide)

_____ copies of the 2s & 3s Student Worksheet

_____ copies of the Bible Lesson for 4s & 5s (Teacher's Guide)

_____ copies of the 4s & 5s Student Worksheet

_____ copies of the Bible Lesson for Grades 1-3 (Teacher's Guide)

_____ copies of the Grades 1-3 Student Worksheet

_____ copies of the Bible Lesson for Grades 4-6 (Teacher's Guide)

_____ copies of the Grades 4-6 Student Worksheet

_____ copies of the Bible Lesson for Junior High (Teacher's Guide)

_____ copies of the Junior High Student Worksheet

_____ copies of the Bible Lesson for High School (Teacher's Guide)

_____ copies of the High School Student Worksheet

_____ copies of the Bible Lesson for Adults (Teacher's Guide)

_____ copies of the Adult Student Worksheet

_____ copies of the Service Notes sheet

_____ copies of the Family Activity Guide. These can be distributed at the Sunday Service. Also, for as many age levels as you choose, they can be distributed after the Bible lessons to children's parents who do not attend the service.

_____ copies of the Prayer Guide. These can be distributed particularly to the shut-ins of your fellowship as well as to anyone wanting to pray for an unreached people group.

_____ copies of the Small Group Study Guide for Leaders

_____ copies of the Small Group Student Worksheet

❏ 4. With your committee and church leadership, plan your order of service for *A Sunday for the World*.

- Scan the Sunday Service guidelines;
- Determine number of participants desired;
- Discuss special music needed;
- Select Scripture readings;
- Discuss ways you'd like to customize the service—adding prayer for an unreached people you've already begun to focus on, specifying the responses you seek, etc.;
- Plan how and when you'll collect the tear-off response sections on the congregation's Service Notes sheet.

❏ 5. Pray.

- Pray for this celebration of God's heart for every people on earth—our own included!
- Pray that your people will be encouraged;
- Pray that many will be, if not eager, at least curious to find out more on these topics of God's global plan;
- Pray for an integration of global and local vision;
- Pray the Lord of the harvest to send forth many from your fellowship into the harvest fields;

• Pray for a new fervency and involvement in prayer throughout your fellowship.

THREE TO FOUR WEEKS BEFORE YOUR *SUNDAY FOR THE WORLD*

☐ 1. Pray.

☐ 2. List the dates and times of your *Sunday for the World* activities in the church's newsletter.

☐ 3. Post your posters on bulletin boards in Sunday School classrooms.

☐ 4. Include one or more of the suggested bulletin announcements in this Sunday's bulletin.

☐ 5. Announce the upcoming *Sunday for the World* in all your usual promotional channels.

☐ 6. If using the Bible Lessons, distribute a Teacher's Guide, the appropriate number of Student Worksheets and Family Activity Guides to each teacher.

☐ 7. If using the Small Group Study Guides and Student Worksheets, distribute to each group leader enough copies for each participant.

☐ 8. Personally deliver a news release (sample enclosed) to every avenue of publicity in your community.

TWO WEEKS BEFORE YOUR *SUNDAY FOR THE WORLD*

☐ 1. Pray. Organize a group to pray for your church's response to the message of A Sunday for the World.

☐ 2. Include more of the suggested bulletin announcements in this Sunday's bulletin.

☐ 3. Photocopy Poster 1 onto acetate to make an overhead transparency. Display this overhead before and after your Sunday services.

☐ 4. Announce the upcoming *A Sunday for the World* through all your usual promotional channels.

☐ 5. Consider setting up a display of maps, globes and travel posters or a table of mission books and materials, a gallery of your church missionaries' photos, a rack of pre-addressed envelopes to encourage writing to your missionaries, or a display of foreign artifacts and curios.

ONE WEEK BEFORE YOUR *SUNDAY FOR THE WORLD*

☐ 1. Pray. Organize a prayer group to volunteer for specific time-slots of prayer during the entire *A Sunday for the World* emphasis.

☐ 2. Post fresh announcements and/or posters on bulletin boards in classrooms.

☐ 3. Photocopy Poster 2 onto acetate to make an overhead transparency. Display this overhead before and after your Sunday services.

☐ 4. Announce the upcoming *A Sunday for the World* in all possible promotional channels. Be creative: For example, perhaps several

international students could go from class to class and announce next week's global emphasis in their native languages. Perhaps this week initiate a phone chain in which every person called then phones three more to invite them to the activities of *A Sunday for the World*.

❑ 5. Check that all Bible Lesson teachers and Small Group Study leaders have adequate materials. Be sure all children's workers have extra copies of the Family Activity Guide for those parents not attending the services.

ON THE DAY OF YOUR *SUNDAY FOR THE WORLD*

❑ 1. Pray. Consider asking all of your fellowship's prayer warriors to meet before any of the events of the day to pray.

❑ 2. The only on-the-job concern you'll have today is being available to make extra photocopies of various sheets if needed.

❑ 3. Enjoy the celebration!

PROMOTIONAL MATERIALS

PROMOTIONAL POSTER 1

- Feel free to create your own promotional posters and materials if the following are not appropriate for your fellowship.
- If you do use the following, photocopy as many sheets as you'll need.
- Consider having a group color the posters. (You'll be surprised how much even an adult group will love to doodle and color these promotional materials.)
- Copy one reproduction onto an acetate sheet to make an overhead transparency. Color this in carefully with overhead pens. Display this poster transparency via the overhead projector before and after meetings and services.

PROMOTIONAL POSTER 2

- Photocopy as many sheets as you'll need.
- Consider having a group color the posters.
- Copy one reproduction onto an acetate sheet to make an overhead transparency. Color this in carefully with overhead pens. Display this poster transparency via the overhead projector before and after meetings and services.

PROMOTIONAL LEAFLETS

- If you'd like, insert your church name and the date of your upcoming *A Sunday for the World* on the following leaflets.
- Photocopy as many sheets as you'll need.
- Use as bulletin inserts, newsletter inserts, handouts after services and meetings, mini-posters, mailers.

NEWS FLASH:

THERE WILL BE BOZOS IN HEAVEN!

FIND OUT MORE AT
A SUNDAY FOR THE WORLD

GOING ABOUT YOUR FATHER'S BUSINESS?

JUST WHAT BUSINESS IS HE IN THESE DAYS?

FIND OUT SOME INTERESTING DETAILS AT
A SUNDAY FOR THE WORLD

EVER FEEL INSIGNIFICANT?

Cheer up. You're one of at least 560 million committed believers in Jesus Christ worldwide. That's not even counting nominal Christians. When we count them (since *some* are true believers who are just not living a Christlike lifestyle), nearly a third of the exploding population on our planet claim Jesus Christ as their personal Lord and Savior. As a believer, you're part of a significant movement.

EVER FEEL OVERLY SIGNIFICANT?

Hate to burst your bubble. But North American believers now make up only about one-tenth of the worldwide Body of Christ. If we limit our relationships in the Body to only North American believers, we're missing 90 percent of what God is doing today. In the past 10 years, 300 million have been added to the Body of Christ worldwide. And just 10 million of those are from the West. We're a definite minority!

(Statistics from the Lausanne Statistical Task Force and the Discipling A Whole Nation—Europe Office.)

FIND OUT MORE DURING OUR UPCOMING *SUNDAY FOR THE WORLD!*

A CELEBRATION OF GOD'S HEART FOR EVERY PEOPLE

We're mixing up a batch of Amazon Basin yeast and Indonesian shoe polish just for you.* Why? Because you need to be at *A Sunday for the World* to catch great true stories such as...

Mombasa, Kenya. Salty, hot evening air wafts along the concrete quay this evening as you sip your iced tea, syrupy with sugar and with no ice. An American sitting across the outdoor table overlooking the bay smiles with the latest report. The summer's unbelievable breakthrough in the city gives you goose bumps even in the humid heat; more than 56,000 Muslims have come to faith in Christ over a three-month period.

"Much of it started," the friend says, "when a little girl was healed in the name of *Isa*—Jesus—at a local mosque. A very important 70-year-old *imam*—a Muslim priest—told me he wanted to read about *Isa*. He wouldn't accept a Bible, of course. So at home that night I asked forgiveness, ripped the covers off a New Testament, stuck on a cardboard cover and wrote *The Teachings of Isa* on it. After he had read and completely memorized it, he received Jesus as Savior and wanted to be baptized. This caused a citywide uproar, of course. And his family said that if he were baptized, they'd kill him. I met with him the day before he was going to be baptized, and he said he wasn't afraid to die for Jesus. He just wished he could first go back as a missionary to his home country and tell all his aged Shi'ite Muslim teachers that Jesus is the Way, the Truth and the Life. His home country is Iran. Not exactly open to former Muslim missionaries." Your friend takes a sip of the heavy tea.

"Well," you say, "what happened?"

"The next morning I went to his family's house and asked for him. His youngest son stepped out and told me he was no longer there. I said, 'You killed him, didn't you?' He said, 'We gathered the entire clan last night to argue with him about this *Isa,* but he wouldn't break. So we did the unthinkable. He is, after all, the head of our clan. We told him he needed to be reeducated in the ways of Islam. We took up a collection and shamefully sent him away....' The young man hung his head. '...Back to Iran.'"

Pray for these thousands of recent converts from Islam now being followed up in discipling groups in Mombasa. And pray for the old former imam as he shares the Truth with some of the leading Islamic teachers of Iran—compliments of the Muslims of Mombasa.

FIND OUT MORE OF
WHAT GOD IS DOING
IN THE WORLD TODAY AT

A SUNDAY FOR THE WORLD

A CELEBRATION OF
GOD'S HEART
FOR EVERY PEOPLE

* It'll help you—ahem—rise and shine!

PROMOTIONAL SAMPLE NEWS RELEASE

- If you can gather even a few members of your fellowship for a photo session, have a serious photographer take several group shots. (Many area newspapers will offer the services of their own photographer.) Try for a mixture of ages and activities—children hanging a globe, elderly and teenagers preparing a foreign dish, members of various ethnic backgrounds laughing with each other, etc.

- Add your own details to one or both of these sample news releases and retype in double-space format. Note that the first release is a simple notification of your upcoming event. The second just might add some spice to your community of churches. Edit as you see fit.

- A month before your Sunday for the World, distribute your releases by mail to all area Christian radio stations and newspaper religion editors.

- Be prepared to answer simple queries from media as they receive the releases.

- Take advantage of any offers of taping your invitation to attend *A Sunday for the World* or of interviewing you or a church leader about what God is doing globally and how local churches can take a more active part. (The Breakthroughs listed for the Sunday Service will provide plenty of fuel for a hot interview.)

News Release Sample 1

Your Church Name

News Release

For Immediate Release

Date

(If applicable) Photo Enclosed

For further information contact: (Name, phone number)

LOCAL CHURCH HOSTS *A SUNDAY FOR THE WORLD*

The _____(fellowship)_____ is presenting *A Sunday for the World*,

a celebration of God's heart for every people, on _____(date)_____. Activities

are planned for each age group beginning at _____(time)_____. The community is invited to

attend. For more information, contact _____(contact persons and numbers)_____.

Your Church name, address and contact numbers.

News Release Sample 2

Your Church Name

News Release

<u>For Immediate Release</u>

Date

(If applicable) Photo Enclosed

For further information contact: (Name, phone number)

LOCAL CHURCH MEETS REAL WORLD

A world where there are more disciples who speak Spanish than English. A world where a white person is seen as coming from the minority world. Where every day another 174,000 become believers in Jesus Christ (Source: Strategic Frontiers, 1994).

Of course, it's the real world, insist members of _____(fellowship)_____, who are hosting *A Sunday for the World* on _____(date)_____. This celebration for all ages is set to encourage local Christians to look at the global spread of true Christianity.

One presentation points out, for example, that many Bible-believing Christians have heard that Islam is the fastest growing religion in the world. While it's true that Islam and Hinduism are both expanding by biological growth alone, biblical Christianity is actually growing the fastest of any world religion. Generally, world population is growing at 1.7 percent while Islam increases at 2.7 percent per year and Hinduism by 2.3 percent. Meanwhile, the planet's population of true, committed believers in Jesus Christ increases at about 6.9 percent per year (Source: *Global Evangelization Movement Database, 1995*).

And almost all that growth is in the Two-Thirds World—the developing countries. True Christianity has become the most diverse of the world's religions, with followers in North America now representing only about 10 percent of the worldwide mass of committed believers in Jesus Christ.

Anyone interested in learning more about the growth and cultural diversity of true Christianity is invited to attend *A Sunday for the World* at _____(location)_____ on Sunday, _____(date and times)_____. Contact the church for details at _____(phones)_____.

Your Church name, address and contact numbers.

BIBLE LESSON OVERVIEW

SUNDAY SERVICE

HEAVEN IS A WONDERFUL PLACE

Revelation 5:9
God has a place for each of us in His great global plan that leads us into eternity. That plan and destiny involve every people group on the face of the earth. The process of the plan starts with God blessing us as His people to in turn bless every people—including our own.

CHURCH LEADERSHIP

WITHOUT A VISION...

Proverbs 29:18
How can a vision for the whole world be integrated with a vision for strengthening our own lives as well as impacting our own culture? Getting scriptural is key to a single, common vision in the church.

FAMILIES

FROM INDIA TO CAIRO

1 Timothy 6:7-11 and Isaiah 19:19-22
Learning about God's heart for every people coaches us to pray against the materialism of the unreached Pakanati Reddis of India and for the fundamentalist Muslims of Cairo.

NURSERY WORKERS

NEXT CENTURY'S HARVEST FORCE

Psalm 67:1,2,7
Little ones in the nursery will grow up in a challenging time of tremendous harvest of souls for God's kingdom.

2s & 3s

JESUS LOVES ALL THOSE CHILDREN

Mark 10:14
Jesus loves all the children of the world.

4s & 5s

BLESSINGS FOR ALL

Psalm 67:1,2

God blesses me so I can bless others.

GRADES 1-3

PARTNERS AND PEOPLES

Genesis 12:2,3

God has chosen to partner with His people. The partnership works as He blesses us and we pass on His blessing to the whole world.

GRADES 4-6

PRIESTS FOR THE PEOPLES

Psalm 67:7

God's people are a nation of priests. And priests have a job to do—interceding for and ministering to the peoples of the world.

JUNIOR HIGH

BOZOS AND ROCKETS

Revelation 5:9

As we understand more clearly what God is doing, we can find our part in His great plan. We'll find our specific role in one of the four basic dynamics of the overall mission of the church.

HIGH SCHOOL

WORLD-CLASS SPECIAL FX

Revelation 5:9

God is wonderfully breaking into people groups worldwide. His blessing of every people is a theme we see throughout Scripture.

ADULT

SPRINT THROUGH THE BIBLE

John 4:35

We can better understand God's work today by recognizing people-group thinking and the principle that we are blessed to bless every people.

SMALL GROUPS

Bible Lesson Overview

IT CAN BE DONE

Acts 2:39
The task of The Great Commission is so huge that most believers see it only as an ideal. But by following God's basic principles illustrated in the early church, we can say, "It can be done!"

PRAYER GUIDE

PRAY FOR THE TURKMEN

Matthew 28:19,20
One of the most powerful things we can do to see some from every people, tribe, tongue and nation in heaven is to pray more specifically.

Leader-
ship
Session

WITHOUT A VISION...

KEY VERSE

"Where there is no vision, the people perish." Proverbs 29:18, *KJV*

KEY BIBLE PASSAGE

1 Chronicles 12:32; Psalm 23:3; 67:1,2; 84:5; Proverbs 29:18; Isaiah 25:6; Matthew 24:14; Luke 19:44; Acts 1:8; 10:38; Ephesians 4:4-6; 1 John 4:1-12; Revelation 5:9; 21:24,26

OVERVIEW

Use the following session as a preliminary meeting to *A Sunday for the World* or as a follow-up, an at-home fellowship, a retreat, etc.

Included are the Session Commentary and "Take-Home Thought-Provoker."

This Leadership Session gears the leaders of your fellowship to think through the integration of local and global vision. Leaders are to read through the Session Commentary before gathering.

The Leadership Session ideally should occur well before the *A Sunday for the World* program, but even scheduling it after the special Sunday will enhance your leadership's outlook on how God may be leading you into more strategic involvement in His global plan.

SESSION COMMENTARY
(TO BE READ BEFORE THE SESSION)

If you're planning toward or debriefing after *A Sunday for the World*, you might feel the frustration of many church leaders when it comes to emphasizing God's global purpose. An imbalanced push toward mission involvement can actually bring disunity in a congregation.

MISSION DIVISION

Among all the competing interest groups in a church, the Unreached Peoples Missions Club can plead for more bulletin space, more budget allotments, more volunteers. Frontier mission fanatics can point long, bony fingers in judgment at other believers in the fellowship and announce that if a Christian doesn't have a personal involvement in reaching an unreached people, he or she just isn't in the will of God. There might be hints that other ministries in the church just aren't as spiritual as missions involvement.

Sometimes mission-minded believers can be obnoxious. Why? Because serious world Christians often don't take the time to think, pray and talk through an integrated vision of the overall mission of their local church. God's heart for every people can be a unifying, empowering and affirming factor in all the ministries of a fellowship.

The biblical theme of God blessing His people to bless every people provides an inspired structure for the overall mission of the church—including a clear emphasis on reaching the unreached nations of the earth.

YOUR CHURCH: THE ROCKET

God blesses His people with health, talents, finances, spiritual gifts, skills and His relationship. And, in the biblical pattern of "Blessed is the nation [the people group] whose God is the Lord," we can joyfully receive God's blessings. We don't need to feel guilty when God pours out His blessing on our lives, our families, our congregation. It's part of what He has promised to do in His plan to demonstrate His character to all the peoples of the world, but the blessing is for a purpose:

> God be gracious unto us and bless us,
>
> And cause His face to shine upon us—
>
> That Thy way might be made known on the earth,
>
> Thy salvation among all nations
>
> (Psalm 67:1,2).

How does this twofold program—being blessed to be a blessing to every people—form a structure for integrating ministries? Think through these illustrations of a rocket as the overall mission of a church. You'll find the fault in this illustration soon enough, but consider the parallels: The local church is like a four-stage rocket.

30

The First Dynamic: God blesses His people to strengthen the local church.

The church is to be strengthened for its task of channeling God's blessing to every people. Children are to be nurtured in the admonition of the Lord, families are to be encouraged and equipped with everything from communication skills to financial management, couples must be counseled, youth discipled, offerings collected, prayers offered in behalf of the fellowship, bodies exercised, sermons preached, walls painted, fellowship enjoyed, buildings built, etc. All the gifts, skills and ministries that go on within the church itself can be affirmed and encouraged because the church needs to be strong for its world-level purpose. This is the power dynamic, the booster stage of the rocket.

The Second Dynamic: The local church is to bless every people group—including its own.

Here's where the church starts impacting the world outside its walls. Here is also where many mission fanatics fail in developing an integrated vision of God's heart for every people. Every people includes our own.

The easiest people group to offer God's blessing to is, of course, a fellowship's own people group. Here are some ways this dynamic of the overall mission of the church can be expressed as salt and light:

- In evangelism: As a church movement is established in a people group, it is that church's obligation to evangelize its own culture. So mass and personal evangelism isn't just one of the compartments of a local church's ministry; sharing the Good News with neighbors is crucial to the global scope of the Great Commission.

- In ministering to community needs: Ministering goodness within a fellowship's own culture isn't simply a matter of being nice. Caring for the homeless, visiting the sick, ministering to those in prison, tending suicide hotlines, giving to the poor, sponsoring an unwed mothers' home, cleaning up trash on the highway, offering free baby-sitting for mothers' days off, raising money for medical research, singing Christmas carols in the mall for the enjoyment of shoppers—all are ways of blessing one's own culture by simply "going about doing good" (see Acts 10:38).

The benefits of living in a community where Christians are consistently, sacrificially doing good makes God's love visible for mankind (see 1 John 4:1-12). God relieves suffering through His people. But further, Christians ministering goodness in the name of Jesus Christ illustrates the character of God for the whole world to see. Besides all that, serious Christian love in action makes a nice place to live for everybody including the Christians.

Caring ministries performed by believers often set the stage for evangelism, and generally allow God's principle to work that "blessed is the people whose God is the Lord"—His blessing affects even unbelievers in an *ethne* through the actions of His people.

- Standing up for righteousness in one's own people group is another ministry category of this second dynamic of the

mission of the church. A church must often bless its own culture the hard way—by taking a stand for God's character on issues. When Christians fight pornography, battle drug and child abuse, crime, corruption and injustice, they not only help bless their own culture. God "guides [us] in paths of righteousness for His name's sake" (Psalm 23:3).

God's name always denotes His character: He is holy, righteous and just. So standing up for His name on issues in a believer's own society isn't only so the streets will be safer and life will be nicer. Blessing one's own culture also broadcasts to every people on earth the character of God. Every ministry of the church pressing for righteousness in society is crucial to the global reputation of a God who doesn't excuse sin.

The Third Dynamic: The local church is to bless every people group including reached peoples.

Here is where the church begins to cross cultural barriers. A reached people is a distinct ethnic group which has a viable church movement capable of evangelizing its own culture. More than half of the people groups on earth are in this category.

A fellowship's ministries in this third stage are cross-cultural—that is, they must bridge language, social or other cultural barriers. It is the job of the church in a reached culture such as the Romanian culture (more than 12 percent evangelical) to bless its own people in evangelism, doing good and standing up for righteousness in its society. So it is more than patronizing when another culture's church—such as an American church—tries to single-handedly do those jobs. It is offensive, since the outside culture is suggesting the people group's church isn't capable of evangelism, doing good or salting its own society.

It is also counter-productive to the pattern of God's global plan, since the church in a reached people will not grow strong if someone else is doing its work. Churches in reached people groups need to be strong (Stage One) because they too have a global, big-picture job to do.

Blessing other reached peoples entails:

- serving their churches;
- empowering them to bless their own culture (their own Stage Two) and to equip other reached peoples (their own Stage Three);
- partnering with them to offer Christ's redemption to unreached peoples.

The Fourth Dynamic: The local church is to bless every people group including the remaining unreached peoples of the world.

Psalm 84:5 says: "How blessed is the man whose strength is in Thee; in whose heart are the highways to Zion!"

There are, stretching out through what will become history, roads that lead to our celestial city—the New Jerusalem—which will house some from every nation: "And the nations shall walk by its light,...and they shall bring the glory and the honor of the nations into it" (Revelation 21:24,26).

Think of these roads as they wind through every last people group on the face of the earth. As we make our pilgrimage as the Church, we

swell our ranks with new believers from one people, then another, then another until we all march into the gates which never close, into this awesome city.

We as the Church in our local churches are heading through every last people group on earth. This is the specific, measurable point—the nose cone that sets the direction—of the overall mission of the Church.

The fourth dynamic of a church is to see that the blessing of redemption is offered to every remaining unreached people group.

This is the realm of frontier, pioneer missions, where the entire Church worldwide can partner to focus its resources. What happens in this stage of the rocket—the Church?

- Pre-Evangelism—relief efforts, Christians winning favor in political, educational or business realms, medical work, etc.— is needed to prepare the way, to establish the reputation of the character of God in Christ among that unreached people.

- Church-Planting—Some unbelievers must come to faith in Christ. Churches must be planted. Those newborn congregations must be discipled to be strengthened, reaching out into their own people and crossing cultural barriers in their own history of being blessed to be a blessing to every people.

AN INTEGRATED VISION

The whole Church, with all its varying parts, functions, giftings and ministries working in unity, goes about the Father's business. We're not just a family; we're a family business. God pours His blessing into us to pass on His blessing in Jesus Christ to the whole world— people group by people group. Our job in the family business—our overall mission—is very specific:

- We're heading toward a specific goal. It's a celestial city called Zion. Some from "every tribe and tongue and people and nation" will gather in the throne room of the Lamb (Revelation 5:9). Billions and billions of humans will enjoy a festival: "The Lord Almighty will prepare a feast of rich food for all peoples" (Isaiah 25:6, NIV). Looking back into time from that dazzling city, we'll see that the grace of God worked through His people in ministries from Jerusalem to the uttermost parts to invite guests from every people to the party.

- There is a specific path to be followed down the "highways to Zion" (Psalm 84:5) with blessing offered to those "who have set their hearts on [this] pilgrimage" (Psalm 84:5, NIV). That highway to Zion leads right through the heart of every unreached people group remaining.

- The identity of these people groups is specific, definable: God has a registry of the peoples (see Psalm 87:6) listing the exact number of those yet to be reached. And we're getting close to a clear reading of that heavenly scroll.

- There is a specific timetable involved in this task. The mission of your church is not a vague program of having lots of meetings and trying to do everything until Jesus returns. The mission of the Church comprises a countdown of the discipling of the world's people groups: "And this gospel of the kingdom

shall be preached in the whole world for a witness to all the nations, and then the end shall come" (Matthew 24:14).

Studying and praying through specifics like these will help you catch a single-minded vision of your part in God's great plan. The direction of your life mission and the mission of your church is a fine line leading:

- from where your feet are right now;
- along a path of ministry that strengthens your church or blesses your people or blesses another people;
- through the spiritual core of a yet-to-be-reached people group;
- to an eternity filled with the diversity of mankind's peoples bringing honor and glory to God.

An integrated vision in a fellowship is not only specific. It is also noncompetitive.

Folks whose interests and ministries concentrate on the nose cone of seeing an unreached people discipled can affirm the other God-given ministries of the fellowship.

These mission fanatics know that frontier mission efforts desperately need a strong power base. So the true mission visionary thinks through how the various home front ministries fit in the overall mission of the church. And missions people become renowned for encouraging and promoting the women's aerobics group, a new building program, a second-grade boys' Sunday School class and fishing trip—and other God-given ministries in the church that on the surface seem to have nothing to do with reaching an unreached people.

An integrated vision in a fellowship is liberating. An integrated, single vision in a local church also frees up the resources of a congregation. How? As a fellowship lists its assets in manpower, prayer power, finances, talents, etc., it invariably realizes its limitations. One church can't do it all.

Let's say a fellowship senses its origins, giftings and interests seem to emphasize the second dynamic of the overall mission of the church. They strengthen their own fellowship in all sorts of ministries so that they can unleash God's blessing on their neighbors, their city, their own culture.

Knowing that evangelism builds the Kingdom army, knowing that standing up for righteousness in our own culture is crucial to a credible message in other cultures, the church buses children, holds training sessions for personal evangelism, prepares lunch sacks for the homeless, visits children's homes, etc.

Now, shouldn't this fellowship also partner with another culture's church? Shouldn't they also focus on reaching an unreached people? Perhaps not. Just as God graces individual believers with varying giftings, He often gives a personality and an area of emphasis to a whole fellowship. As that fellowship submits to the authority of the Head of the Body, God aligns the giftings of that church into His overall plan.

A church needs to acknowledge and in prayer be especially concerned with each of the four dynamics of the Church. But not every church needs to feel pressured to do everything, to spread its limited resources too thin, to run ministries simply because all the growing churches are doing this. As uncomfortable as it may sound to frontier

mission zealots, not every church should commit itself to planting a church in an unreached people.

When a congregation knows what it's about, knows which areas of the mission of the Church are its forte, the pressure is off. Pastors and elders and even mission committee members are guilt-free to say, "That's a great ministry idea, but we don't have the resources for it because this is where we're headed...."

Meanwhile, this freedom to emphasize a church's strengths makes networking between churches all the more important. Let's say Church A, whose specialty is blessing its own people, launches a neighborhood ministry. Perhaps it encounters families who come from another culture. But because cross-cultural church-planting is known to be Church B's specialty, Church A blesses the efforts of Church B as it (B) takes the ball and works to plant a church among the families of that other culture. Church B benefits from the pre-evangelism done by Church A, and Church A is relieved of a ministry it's not equipped to handle. The various parts of the Body complement each other. What a concept!

A unifying vision can be specific, non-competitive and liberating.

MALFUNCTIONS IN THE MISSION

We believers can enjoy a single, unifying, integrated vision and our part in it. The image of the rocket representing the mission of the Church is, of course, faulty because being blessed to bless every people is not a chronological process. That brings us to the first of the possible malfunctions in our mission:

- Sometimes we think that any attention paid to the uttermost parts of the earth has to wait until we've first perfected our Jerusalems, Judeas and Samarias. Although it's true that the Stage One blessing-strengthening of the local church is foundational to ministry, it's not true that we can't concern ourselves with other cultures until our own is fully redeemed. Jesus told us to be witnesses simultaneously in Jerusalem, Judea, Samaria and the uttermost parts of the earth (see Acts 1:8).

- Another malfunction in our mission can be getting stuck in Stage One. A fellowship which concentrates on strengthening itself for the sake of strengthening itself is like a body builder who pumps up and pumps up his muscles until he can hardly move.

A church that concentrates only on Stage One is like the powerful booster stage of a rocket with no place to go. The first stage blasts into action and careens in every direction like a deflating balloon. A church with no clear direction but lots of activity diffuses its resources; the people tire of activity and suffer burnout. Ministry activity—virtually all within the fellowship—is furious, but the fruit of ministry is sparse.

Without a clear vision of their overall mission, of where they're heading, the people lose discipline. Without a vision, the people lose focus. They, as the *King James Version* puts it, perish (see Proverbs 29:18).

- Another malfunction of our single-vision mission is neglect of Stage One. A fellowship might concentrate on blessing an unreached people but neglect strengthening its base. That

congregation might be like a needle-nosed rocket nose cone floating wonderfully through space—with no thrust.

- Often mission activist groups feel a clear sense of purpose and direction, but they are frustrated by lack of prayer power, financial power and manpower. In frustration, these folks begin to point fingers at the lack of vision of the pastor, the elders or the rest of the congregation for their obvious selfishness.

- Or a mission-minded church might malfunction by failing to impact its own culture in Stage Two. What, then, gives it a right to tell an unreached people "blessed is the people whose God is the Lord"?

For example: You're sent from your hometown by a consortium of five churches to help reach the Buryat Mongolians, a people living in the Siberian stretches of Russia just north of Mongolia. In the regional capital of Ulan-Ude, you sit down with the elder political leaders of the city. They ask, "We do not worship your Christian God. Why should we allow you to stir up our citizens about Jesus Christ?"

You say, "In my hometown, the Christians have declared our city to be a 'hunger-free zone.' They're seeing to it that no one in our city goes hungry ever again. Would you like to see that happen here in Ulan-Ude? In my neighborhood, Christians have developed a job training center for young people. Would you like several of these across your city? All the Christians in my town are helping solve problems of alcoholism and lack of child care for working mothers. They're helping people learn to read and are caring for the elderly.

"There are Christian businessmen and women in my home city who have been sharpening their skills for years as they helped bless my town. Some have said they will come to Ulan-Ude to teach seminars on starting new businesses. Others will help you receive grant funding from international foundations to create more jobs. Still others have volunteered to serve as consultants for your efforts to export your freshwater fish products and to develop energy sources. And all this will cost you nothing. We come to serve you in the name of Jesus Christ just as we serve our own people."

You conclude: "Because Jesus Christ tells His followers to bless every people, we want to bless the Buryat people of Ulan-Ude."

Imagine the city fathers frowning at your offer: "And will you at the same time be telling them about Christianity? We are not Christians here; we are atheists and some are Buddhists."

You reply, "We could have an agreement: We will do our very best to bless the Buryat people. If anyone asks why we are doing these things, may we tell them about Jesus Christ?"

The elders turn to each other slowly, faces inscrutable. Finally one says—speaking English for the first time without translation—"Okay."

A church with a vision of its mission that reaches to the uttermost parts of the earth must have a strong Stage Two. Fulfilling your obligation to bless your own culture gives the credibility that too often missionary enterprises lack in offering God's blessing to an unreached people.

Besides, if a local fellowship isn't evangelizing its own community, it simply won't be growing enough prayer power, manpower and other

36

resources to be effective in the big picture; no new believers in the church is a sure sign of a malfunction. A mission-minded church that isn't activating its local ministries is destined to talk big but accomplish little in God's great global enterprise.[1]

A SUNDAY FOR THE WORLD

As you church leaders think, discuss and pray through God's big-picture plans for your future, be vigilant to preserve the unity of your local body of believers. Encourage them toward a single, unified vision of their purpose.

A Sunday for the World isn't just for the mission fanatics. It's a program to inspire the vision of the entire congregation. After all, we aren't just a conglomeration of competing interest groups. We are one body called in one hope, with one Lord, one faith, one baptism, one God and Father (see Ephesians 4:4-6). It would certainly make sense that we catch a clear vision of how our diverse ministries can be integrated in the overall mission of our church.

1. Material adapted from *Run With the Vision* by Bob Sjogren and Bill and Amy Stearns; Bethany House, 1995.)

LESSON PLAN

A minimum time of one hour required for session.

MATERIALS REQUIRED

- Bibles
- Photocopies of the Session Commentary (to be read before the session)
- Photocopies of the "Take-Home Thought-Provoker"
- White board, chalkboard, flipchart or large sheet of paper and markers

SESSION AT A GLANCE

Opening Prayer (5-10 minutes)

Ministry Survey (15-20 minutes)

Discussion (30 minutes)

Closing Prayer Time (Open-Ended)

THE SESSION

OPENING PRAYER (5-10 MINUTES)

Pray for each other—perhaps going around the circle. Center your prayers on seeing God's vision for your fellowship. The sons of Issachar "understood their times, [and knew] what Israel should do" (1 Chronicles 12:32) while many leaders of Jesus' earthly lifetime "did not recognize the time of [their] visitation" (Luke 19:44).

MINISTRY SURVEY (15-20 MINUTES)

Have your resident artist draw the rocket describe in the Session Commentary on a chalkboard, whiteboard, flipchart or a large piece of paper.

Brainstorm to list all the official and unofficial ministries going on in and through your church.

Decide which stage each ministry impacts and list it on that part of the rocket.

DISCUSSION (30 MINUTES)

Choose a reporter to jot general notes and a moderator to enforce the following discussion guidelines:

- No one speaks for more than two minutes at a time.
- Everyone is encouraged to participate.
- No interruptions are allowed.

- Comments and discussion on related topics are allowed, but keep coming back to how the congregation can enjoy a single vision of their mission as a church.

Be sure everyone has read through the Session Commentary. If not, allow extra time for that reading. Then talk through some of the following statements. Feel free to add your own discussion items.

Agree or Disagree	1. We're trying to do too many things.
Agree or Disagree	2. The distribution of our ministries in the various stages of the rocket is about the way we want it.
Agree or Disagree	3. This "blessed to bless every people" is a fair overview of our mission as it includes strengthening our home base, blessing our own people as well as other people groups.
Agree or Disagree	4. Most of our people can verbalize our overall mission as a church.
Agree or Disagree	5. Missions is seen as a separate compartment in the life of our church.
Agree or Disagree	6. Missions has had a divisive effect on our church.
Agree or Disagree	7. Being "blessed to bless every people" is a good framework for infusing our members with the idea of a common vision.

CLOSING PRAYER TIME (OPEN-ENDED)

Feel free to kneel together. Mix personal prayer requests with petitions for the church as a whole. Spend as much time in prayer together as you can. Pass out the "Take-Home Thought-Provoker" to each participant.

TAKE-HOME THOUGHT-PROVOKER

Jesus Christ might return now. Or He may wait another hundred years. Or more. So let's be sure to think long-range in our vision. How might the following concept affect the big-picture vision of your fellowship in the coming decades?

- The beginning of the Church was at the east end of the Mediterranean. The virtual center of gravity of the Church was in Jerusalem, and the force of God's power through the Church radiated from there.

- After a few hundred years, the focus of God's power seemed to move westward to Rome. Most—not all, but most—of the Church's expansion radiated from there.

- Several hundred years later, the focal point of the Body of Christ seemed to move westward again—to Western Europe. And for centuries, the blessing of God and the power of the Spirit rested on that area. The force of the Church radiated out particularly from England to the rest of the world.

- Then westward it moved yet again. The focus of the power of the Church—the place of particular blessing—seemed to become North America. And for nearly two hundred years, the blazing impact of the Church of Jesus Christ emanated most brightly from that part of the world. It's not that God was not active in other areas. But there seemed to be a special ease of grace pouring into and out of North American ministry.

- And now? Several knowledgeable world-watchers recently have stated that in their estimation, the focus of God's power has lately moved westward again—to the Church in the Pacific Rim and Asia. With the sheer numbers of believers in China running beyond 80 million, with the strategic mission sense of the Church in Singapore, with the prayer focus and zeal of Korean believers and Solomon islanders, with the mission movement across New Zealand, with Papua New Guinea sending out its first missionaries and with a Great Awakening gaining momentum in Australia, the virtual center of gravity of the worldwide Body of Christ is now in east Asia and the Pacific Rim. (The coincidental economic growth of this region is obvious.)

- What about the future? Not as a prophecy, but as a what-if scenario, the cycle could continue. What if, with the return of Hong Kong to the control of the Peoples Republic of China, not just the borders of Hong Kong but of the entire country open more widely to international trade and travel? This could mean more international believers—particularly business professionals—and Bible training materials already have legal access into China. More significantly, it would mean that the powerful Church of believers in China could explode across those borders with the gospel. Where could these millions of tough, committed Christians go with their message? East is the Pacific, so it would make sense that they burst forth westward, discipling the nations of South Asia and the Middle East. And perhaps the cycle would then one day be completed—as the focus of God's power in the Church returns again to Jerusalem.

What implications might this what-if concept have—

- On your church's outreach training?

- On the schooling and careers recommended to your youth? On the relationships you cultivate with mission agencies and missionary teams?

- On your expectations of the receptivity of North American society in the future (considering Western Europe's current reluctance to embrace a vibrant Christianity)?

- On the significance of international students studying in North America—the majority of whom are now Asians?

NEXT CENTURY'S HARVEST FORCE

One of the themes our church is studying today is: "We're blessed to be a blessing to all peoples." This theme is summarized in Psalm 67:

"God be gracious to us and bless us,

And cause His face to shine upon us—

That Thy way may be known on the earth,

Thy salvation among all nations. . . .

God blesses us,

That all the ends of the earth may fear Him"

(Psalm 67:1,2,7).

God's heart is for all peoples, and He has chosen to offer His blessing to them through God's people.

The Lord of the Harvest is moving across the earth in unprecedented ways today. (Be sure to get in on as many *A Sunday for the World* reports as you can to find out what God is doing in our world.)

While you're rocking babies and wiping noses today, enjoy your role as guardian of next century's Harvest Force. These infants are the warriors of the future.

If the Lord delays His Return, the little ones entrusted to you during this *A Sunday for the World* will grow up in a challenging time, a time of tremendous harvest of souls for God's kingdom. So during your time with these little ones...

- Pray; as you hold or watch each child, pray something such as,

"Lord, bring this little one close to You. May she or he be known as Your servant in the challenging days ahead."

- Pray for the infants among the world's remaining unreached people groups. Those children have no one to pray for them since their culture is unreached by the gospel.
- Send home with each child a Family Activity Guide to promote parents' awareness of the principle that we're blessed to pass on God's blessing to every people.

Thank God for the global significance of your nursery work. Ministering to these children and their parents fills a critical, significant need in strengthening our church for its big-picture purpose:

- You're needed to pray for these children who are God's workers for the future harvest.
- You're needed to show what it means to be a blessing to the non-Christian parents of some of your children. "Blessed to be a blessing to every people" includes our own people group. By demonstrating Christlike values in your care and in simply doing good to non-Christian parents, you're blessing them—a critical part of the big picture of the mission of our church.
- You're needed to free parents for Bible study, worship, prayer and fellowship. Why? So they can be equipped for ministry. The job of these parents may be:
  — like your ministry, to help strengthen the church itself, or
  — to help bless our own people in personal evangelism, in standing up for God's sake on issues, in ministering good in the name of Jesus, or
  — to help bless another people which already has a church movement so we can partner together, or
  — to offer God's blessing to every remaining unreached people group.

You're part of God's blessing to our church so that "the ends of the earth may fear Him." Your ministry is vital.

2s & 3s

JESUS LOVES ALL THOSE CHILDREN

KEY VERSE

"Let the little children come to me."

Mark 10:14, *NIV*

KEY BIBLE WORDS

Jesus loves all the children of the world.

AIMS

By the end of today's *A Sunday for the World* session, your older children will be able to:

- Know that Jesus loves children no matter what.
- Feel good about Jesus' love for them.
- Tell family members, "Jesus loves all the children."

LESSON COMMENTARY

This Sunday every age group in the church will catch a fresh vision of what God is doing in the world. Your preschoolers can help reinforce that vision as they take home and show their materials to family members, and as they ask parents to use the Family Activity Guide.

Be sure you yourself don't miss the excitement of God's global plan; if you can't possibly attend the *A Sunday for the World* service itself, be sure to ask for a cassette tape of the message. It's just that important in your continuing, essential ministry to your little ones.

Why is children's ministry so important? From now till the year 2020, world population will continue to zoom. There'll be more than four billion more humans on the face of the planet. Imagine: *Four billion babies!*

Half of the billion Muslims in the world are age 16 and under. Often in the developing countries of the Two-Thirds Word, the majority of a population is made up of children. And—here's the good news—this is exactly the part of the world where the Body of Christ is growing like wildfire!

Jesus loves all those children. And our own children can grow up with a broad sense of their link to Christians worldwide as brothers and sisters in Jesus. Particularly in the future, the most obvious mark of true believers must be their love: "By this all [worldwide] will know that you are My disciples, if you have love for one another" (John 13:35). How can your children love? "We love, because He first loved us" (1 John 4:19). Immersing your little ones in the love of God will prepare them for a world that desperately needs love.

2s & 3s

For Further Personal Study on God's Global Plan

- Read through the globe-trotting Bible study *Catch the Vision 2000* by Bill and Amy Stearns (Bethany House). Available at Christian bookstores or call 800-MISSION.

For Further Mission Vision Materials for Children

- Contact Kids Can Make A Difference, 4445 Webster Drive, York, PA 17402; Phone: 800-543-7554. Request a KidsCan Network Catalog with its up-to-date listing of mission resources for children. To join a computer network of adults who work with children's mission materials and ideas, find someone in your fellowship with a computer and a modem. Have her or him subscribe to this free network for you. Send an e-mail message to:

    kidscan@xc.org

    Leave the "subject" area blank or hit the space bar. Put in the message area: *Subscribe kids-can-net* and add your e-mail address. You'll automatically begin receiving information on networking and on the best mission materials for children.

LESSON PLAN

Note: Much of the following material was adapted from lessons by Kathy Felty, a KidsCan associate.

PREPARATION

1. Pray that the children you minister to will grow up to be strong salt and light, demonstrating God's love—especially across cultural lines—in an increasingly complicated world.

2. Consider having as a permanent part of your classroom equipment a squeezeable or inflatable globe (available at school supply stores), or post a world map. Although the children have no concept of the world, a map or globe can help remind you and your preschoolers that there are children all over the world who have never heard of Jesus Christ.

3. Plan to perform the snack skit with one other teacher or assistant.

4. Prepare materials as noted in the box.

MATERIALS NEEDED

- A photocopy of the Family Activity Guide for each child;
- Photocopies of the "Children of the World" worksheet—the worksheet has enough figures for four children, so copy as many as you'll need;
- Mission magazines (old issues of your church's mission magazines are fine) or other magazines or books featuring photos of other cultures. For the houses in the World Bible Learning Activity, you'll need old magazines from which you can cut photos depicting small ($1\frac{1}{2}$ inches or less) faces of people—especially children—from other cultures;
- Paper lunch sack for each child;

- Newspapers or other scrap stuffing material;
- Construction paper;
- Craft sticks (Popsicle™ sticks);
- Scissors, crayons, glue sticks, stapler;
- For snacks skit: old dress-up clothes, torn clothes, a white robe or sheet, stick-on stars or washable makeup;
- Snacks.

SESSION AT A GLANCE

Adapt the following to your usual routines:

Bible Learning Activities (20-25 Minutes)

Houses for the World
Book Corner
All the Children of the World

Bible Story (8-10 Minutes)

Relaxing Time (10-15 Minutes)

Together for Songs and Fun (10-15 Minutes)

THE SESSION

BIBLE LEARNING ACTIVITIES (20-25 MINUTES)

If any children arrive early, provide skill toys such as shape puzzles, coloring books, etc.

Each teacher leads one of the following activities to help children talk about and practice Bible truths. Or, if you're teaching on your own, choose which one to use and in which order you will lead each segment.

Houses for the World

Materials Needed:

One paper lunch sack per child, construction paper, glue, crayons, stapler, newspapers or other scrap stuffing material, cut out faces of various cultures from magazines—two or three for each child.

Preparation:

Cut various colors of construction paper into 2-inch squares for windows. Have construction paper available to make roofs. The square roof pieces are sized according to the size of the lunch sacks. (See drawing below.)

Activity:

The child draws and colors a door on the front of an unopened lunch sack. Then he or she glues on squares for windows, and glues onto the windows some of the faces. After opening the sacks, the child stuffs it with newspaper scraps so it will stand. More windows may be glued and more doors colored onto the sides and back of the paper bag house.

Close the top of the bag, fold a square of construction paper over

it, and staple to form a roof. (See the following.)

Teaching Talk:

Allow the children to do as much of the house-building as they can. As you work, talk about:

- **Some houses in the world are not tall like these houses. They are long and low—sometimes with no windows at all. What kind of home do you live in? A house like this? An apartment?**
- **Some children live in houses with flat roofs and some with pointed roofs.**

As children complete their houses, open your Bible and talk about:

- **Jesus loves children who live in all kinds of houses.**
- **Show me the faces you're gluing into the windows of your houses. Jesus loves that person. What is that little girl like? Jesus loves her, too. Point to someone who Jesus loves.**
- **The Bible tells us that Jesus loves all the children of the world.**

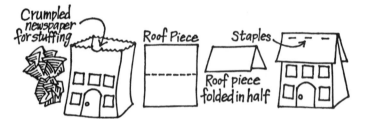

Book Corner

Materials Needed:

Children's books, mission magazines.

Preparation:

Cut a peephole, about a 2-inch circle, from the middle of a sheet of construction paper.

Activity:

Sit with children and leaf through books and magazines. Periodically hold the construction paper over a picture, allowing the children to talk about what they see through the peephole.

Teaching Talk:

Use the peephole paper to encourage curiosity and imagination. Is this a mommy or a child? What do you think this yellow color is? What do you think this picture is about? As you look at pictures, open your Bible and talk about:

- **That girl has black hair. Jesus loves girls with black hair.**
- **This man looks really sad. Maybe he doesn't know Jesus loves him.**
- **That boy looks silly. Do you think Jesus loves boys even when they're silly? When they look different? When they don't have clean clothes on? The Bible says that Jesus wants all the little children to come to Him.**

2" hole cut out of middle of sheet of paper

All the Children of the World

Materials Needed:

The "Children of the World" worksheet, craft sticks, crayons, glue

Preparation:

Photocopy enough "Children of the World" worksheets for your class.

Activity:

Children color their Children of the World figures. Fold their figures for them. Then they glue the figures over craft sticks to make stick puppets. Sing while they work and, as they complete their puppets, lead them in singing while showing their Children of the World.

Cut apart — Fold in half — Craft stick

Some songs you might sing include:

"Jesus Loves the Little Children"

"Praise Him, Praise Him All You Little Children"

"Happy Children" (to the tune of "Did You Ever See a Lassie?")

Happy children who love Jesus, love Jesus, love Jesus,

Happy children who love Jesus go this way and that. (do an action*)

Go this way and that way, go this way and that way.

Happy children who love Jesus go this way and that.

* Twist right/left, bend knees/stand straight, stretch arms up/touch toes, etc.

"Here, There, Everywhere" (to the tune of "Row, Row, Row Your Boat")

Here, there, everywhere, (Point down, point out; then point out with both hands.)

All around the world, (Draw a circle in the air.)

Jesus loves the little ones, (Point up; holds hands over heart.)

Every boy and girl. (Point to a boy, then a girl.)

Cleanup

Several minutes before the Bible story, go to each activity area and tell children that it is now time to clean up. Tell them where to go when cleanup is completed.

BIBLE STORY (8-10 MINUTES)

Gather children to your Bible story area, commenting on how hard they worked or how well they sang during the Bible learning activities.

Hold open the Bible (to Mark 10:14). **In our Bible, Jesus said, "Let the little children come to Me." Jesus loves all the boys and girls of the world. Jesus loves Josiah. Jesus loves Maria, etc.) One day Jesus' helpers said,** (very gruffly) **"Take these children away. Jesus doesn't want them here!" But Jesus said, "Oh, no. Let the little children come to Me."**

(Let another teacher be a disciple. Or act out both parts yourself, being "Jesus" when you sit and a disciple when you stand.) **One of Jesus' helpers might say, "Jeremy and Shawna, stand up."** (They stand.) **"We don't want you here. Go away!" But Jesus says** (patting each), **"Oh, no. I don't want them to go away. I love Jeremy and Shawna. You may sit down now." One of Jesus' helpers might say, "Leroy and Elia, stand up."** (Repeat scene.)

(Hold up some of the Children of the World stick puppets the children have made.) **Jesus loves children who live far, far away. Here's Togo. Jesus loves him. Here's Ti Lynn. Jesus love her.** (Repeat with other stick puppets.)

Pray, thanking Jesus that He loves all the children of the world.

RELAXING TIME (10-15 MINUTES)

Take children to the restroom a few at a time while other children sing songs, work with skill toys or help prepare snack supplies. Be sure each child as well as teacher washes her or his hands.

SNACKS AND SKIT

Skit Preparation

If you have a large group, divide them into five smaller groups and dress a representative of each group with the following. If a small class, dress each child in one of the following costumes:

- Put big shoes (provided by teachers) over their shoes;
- Decorate their cheeks with stick-on stars or washable spots;
- Dress them in outlandish clothing—loud shirts, funny hats;
- Dress them in ripped clothing;

Direct children to sit on the floor.

Skit

Dress in a white robe or sheet and tell the children you'll pretend you're Jesus. Have your coactor bring a tray of snacks. As you begin to serve the first group from the tray, tell them not to eat till after you pray.

Your coactor says **Oh, Jesus, don't give them snacks. They have such big feet!**

You answer **That doesn't matter. I love all the people of the world.**

Oh, Jesus, don't give them snacks. They have funny looking faces.

Again you answer **That doesn't matter. I love all the people of the world.** And so on through your coactor's complaints that they have funny clothes, that they're too poor, etc.

Emphasize that Jesus loves all the people of the world. Then pray, asking His blessing on the snack and thanking Him for loving all of us.

TOGETHER FOR SONGS AND FUN (10-15 MINUTES)

Choose from the following optional activities:

Stretching Time

Some children live far, far away in the world. Let's take a trip and visit them. Lead the children around the world. Climb high mountains, sit in rows on the floor to fly in airplanes, squish together in buses, etc. Stop to stretch out and sleep at night, eat funny food and, most important, meet some of the stick puppet figures who are the children of the world.

Songs

Sing favorite songs especially including action songs. (See song suggestions in the Children for the World Bible Learning Activity at the beginning of the lesson plan.)

Bible Review

Hold Bible open. Say **Jesus said, "Let the little children come to me." He wants all the children of the world to come to Him because He loves every boy and girl. Joshua, point to someone who Jesus loves. How about Tony? Point to Tony. Jesus loves Tony. Now Tony, you point to someone Jesus loves.** (Repeat.)

Bible Learning Activities

Feel free according to your schedule to offer again the activities offered earlier:

- Houses for the World
- Book Corner
- All the Children of the World

Photographs

Hold up magazine photos of faces from various cultures. **What is this man doing? Can you do that? Who do you think loves him? Jesus loves this man. Doesn't this boy look silly? Jesus still loves him.** Repeat.

Pass out each child's handwork and a Family Activity Guide as she or he leaves.

THE CHILDREN OF THE WORLD

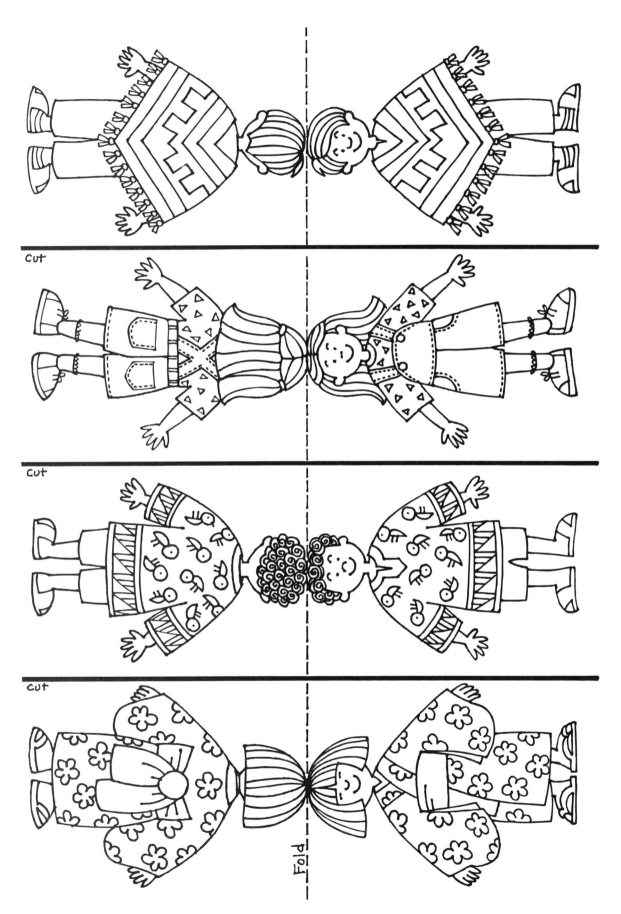

cut

cut

cut

Fold

BLESSINGS FOR ALL

KEY VERSE

"God...bless us...that your ways may be known."
Psalm 67:1,2, *NIV*

KEY BIBLE WORDS

God blesses me so I can bless others.

AIMS

By the end of this *A Sunday for the World* session, your children can:

- Know that God blesses us to bless others.
- Feel that you as adults want to bless them.
- Tell family members, "God blesses me so I can bless others."

LESSON COMMENTARY

This Sunday every age group in the church will catch a fresh vision of what God is doing in the world. Your students can help reinforce that vision as they take home their Student Worksheets to tell their families what they did in class, and to ask their parents to use the Family Activity Guide.

Be sure you yourself don't miss the excitement of God's global plan; if you can't possibly attend the *A Sunday for the World* service itself, be sure to ask for a cassette taping of the message. It's just that important in your continuing, essential ministry to your little ones.

KIDS FOR THE WORLD

Why is children's ministry so important? From now till the year 2020, world population will continue to zoom. There'll be more than four billion more humans on the face of the planet. Imagine: *Four billion babies!*

Half of the billion Muslims in the world are age 16 and under. Often in the developing countries of the Two-Thirds World, the majority of a population is made up of children. And—here's the good news—this is exactly the part of the world where the Body of Christ is growing like wildfire!

God's plan is to offer the blessing of redemption in Jesus Christ to all of these boys and girls. And He works through His people to do this: He blesses us to bless the nations.

4s & 5s

God bless us and be gracious to us
And make Your face to shine upon us
That Your way may be known on earth,
Your salvation among all peoples
(see Psalm 67:1,2, paraphrased).

BLESSED TO BLESS

What is a blessing? The Old Testament word is used of a camel kneeling before its owner; it is "bending the knee." A blessing is given by:

1. Kneeling in honor and humility before the one to be blessed.
2. Establishing a personal relationship with the person. This was demonstrated by holding the person's leg or hand.
3. Stating future benefits about the person.
4. Committing to involvement in seeing those benefits occur.

Apply this to blessing the nations—our own included—and we get a good idea of how to pass on God's blessing to those in our world. Apply this to God's blessing of us, and you get goose bumps: Imagine the God of the universe *kneeling before you,* touching you, stating His promises for your future welfare and committing Himself to seeing those promises become a reality.

Wouldn't it be wonderful if these youngsters were to grow up with a matter-of-fact understanding that as God blesses us, we can bless others? Selfishness is a natural tendency in children, and yet even in a me-first culture, they can learn that God blesses us to bless others in every people—our own included!

For Further Study

- Read through the globe-trotting Bible study *Catch the Vision 2000* by Bill and Amy Stearns (Bethany House). Available at Christian bookstores or call 800-MISSION.

For Further Mission Vision Materials for Children

- Contact Kids Can Make a Difference, 4445 Webster Drive, York, PA 17402; Phone: 800-543-7554. Request a KidsCan Network Catalog with its up-to-date listing of mission resources for children. To join a computer network of adults who work with children's mission materials and ideas, find someone in your fellowship with a computer and a modem. Have her or him subscribe to this free network for you. Send an e-mail message to:

  kidscan@xc.org

  Leave the "subject" area blank or hit the space bar. Put in the message area: *Subscribe kids-can-net* and add your e-mail address. You'll automatically begin receiving information on networking and on the best mission materials for children.

LESSON PLAN

Note: Much of the following material was adapted from lessons by Kathy Felty, a KidsCan associate. (See above for contact information.)

PREPARATION

1. Pray that the children you minister to will grow up to be strong salt and light, demonstrating God's love—especially across cultural lines—in an increasingly complicated world.

2. In your classroom, post a world map for this special emphasis. Consider leaving it up to remind you and your preschoolers that there are children all over the world who have never heard of Jesus Christ.

3. Plan to perform the snack skit with one other teacher or assistant.

4. Prepare materials as noted in the box.

MATERIALS NEEDED

- A photocopy of the Family Activity Guide for each child;
- Photocopies of the "Children of the World" worksheet on page 57; the sheet has enough figures for four children, so copy as many as you'll need;
- Mission magazines (old issues of your church's mission magazines are fine) or other magazines or books featuring photos of other cultures; for the houses in the World Bible Learning Activity, you'll need old magazines from which you can cut photos depicting small (1½ inches or less) faces of people—especially children—from other cultures;
- Paper lunch sack for each child;
- Newspapers or other scrap stuffing material;
- Construction paper;
- Craft sticks (Popsicle™ sticks);
- Scissors, crayons, glue sticks, stapler;
- For snack skit: old dress-up clothes, torn clothes, a white robe or sheet, stick-on stars or washable makeup;
- Snacks.

SESSION AT A GLANCE

Adapt the following to your usual routines:

Bible Learning Activity Options (20-25 Minutes)

Houses for the World

Book Corner

All the Children of the World

Bible Story (10-15 Minutes)

Relaxing Time (5-10 Minutes)

Together for Songs and Fun (10-15 Minutes)

THE SESSION

BIBLE LEARNING ACTIVITIES (20-25 MINUTES)

If any children arrive early, provide skill toys such as shape puzzles, coloring books, etc.

Each teacher leads one of the following opening activities to help children talk about and practice Bible truths. Or, if you're teaching on your own, choose which ones and in which order you'll lead each segment.

Houses for the World

Materials Needed:

One paper lunch sack per child, construction paper, glue, crayons, stapler, newspapers or other scrap stuffing material, cut out faces of various cultures from magazines—two or three for each child.

Preparation:

Cut various colors of construction paper into 2-inch squares for windows. Have construction paper available to make roofs. The square roof pieces are sized according to the size of the lunch sacks. (See the following drawing.)

Activity:

The child draws and colors a door on the front of an unopened lunch sack. Then he or she glues on squares for windows, and glues onto the windows some of the faces. After opening the sacks, the child stuffs it with newspaper scraps so it will stand. More windows may be glued and more doors colored onto the sides and back of the paper bag house.

Close the top of the bag, fold a square of construction paper over it, and staple to form a roof. (See the following drawing.)

Teaching Talk:

Allow the children to do as much of the house-building as they can. As you work, talk about:

- **Some houses in the world are not tall like these houses. They are long and low—sometimes with no windows at all. What kind of home do you live in? A house like this? An apartment?**
- **Some children live in houses with flat roofs and some with pointed roofs.**

As children complete their houses, open your Bible to Psalm 67 and talk about:

- **God blesses us with wood, stones and metal so we can build houses.**
- **Some people in the world don't have houses. How could we bless them?**
- **Show me the faces you're gluing into the windows of your houses. God wants to bless that person. What is that little girl like? God wants to bless her, too.**
- **The Bible tells us that God blesses us so we can bless others who live all over the world.**

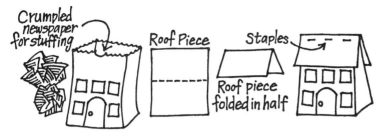

Book Corner

Materials Needed:

Children's books, mission magazines.

Preparation:

Cut a peephole, about a 2-inch circle, from the middle of a sheet of construction paper.

Activity:

Sit with children and leaf through books and magazines. Periodically hold the construction paper over a picture, allowing the children to talk about what they see through the peephole.

Teaching Talk:

Use the peephole paper to encourage curiosity and imagination. Is this a mommy or a child? What do you think this yellow color is? What do you think this picture is about? As you look at pictures, open your Bible and talk about:

- **That girl has black hair. God has blessed her with black hair.**
- **This man looks really sad. Maybe he doesn't know God wants to bless him.**
- **That boy looks silly. Do you think God loves boys even when they're silly? When they look different? When they don't have clean clothes on? The Bible says that God wants to bless all the people of the world.**

All the Children of the World

Materials Needed:

The "Children of the World" worksheet, craft sticks, crayons, glue.

Preparation:

Photocopy enough sheets of the "Children of the World" for your class.

Activity:

Children color their Children of the World figures. Fold their figures for them. Then they glue the figures over craft sticks to make stick puppets. Sing while they work and, as they complete their puppets, lead them in singing while showing their Children of the World.

Some songs you might sing include:

"Jesus Loves the Little Children"
"Praise Him, Praise Him All You Little Children"

"Happy Children"
(To the tune of "Did You Ever See a Lassie?")
Happy children who love Jesus, love Jesus, love
    Jesus,
Happy children who love Jesus go this way and
    that (do an action*).
Go this way and that way, go this way and that
    way.
Happy children who love Jesus go this way and
    that.

* Twist right/left, bend knees/stand straight, stretch arms up/touch
toes, etc.

"Here, There, Everywhere"
(To the tune of "Row, Row, Row Your Boat")
Here, there, everywhere, (Point down, point out;
    then point out with both hands.)
All around the world, (Draw a circle in the air.)
God blesses us to bless, (Point up; holds hands
    over heart.)
Every boy and girl. (Point to a boy, then a girl.)

Cleanup

Several minutes before the Bible story, go to each activity area and tell children that it is now time to clean up. Tell them where to go when cleanup is completed.

BIBLE STORY (8-10 MINUTES)

Gather children to your Bible story area, commenting on how hard they worked or how well they sang during the Bible Learning Activities.

Open your Bible to Psalm 67. Say **God wants to bless us so that we can bless others all around the world. But what does it mean to bless? Let me show you.**

(Be sure to have reviewed the steps of blessing listed in your Lesson Commentary. And prepare yourself for—suddenly—how emotionally serious this demonstration might feel.)

- Invite a child to come to the front.
- Kneel before the child. Hold his hand.
- Look into the child's eyes and pause for just a few seconds while silently asking the Lord for how He wants to bless this child. Then say what comes to your mind. You might be surprised!
- Tell the child how you'll help see these nice things happen in his life. (One way to involve yourself in seeing this blessing happen is to pray for him later today, or for half an hour this week, or every day this week, etc.)

With other teachers and helpers, bless the other children of your class. Have one adult free to sit quietly with those who have gone through the blessing demonstration.

Say **Wasn't that nice? That's what God does to us:**

- **He blesses us by honoring us and telling us we're very important to Him.**
- **He blesses us by holding us tight.**
- **He says nice things about us.**
- **And He helps those nice things to happen.**

The Bible tells us that God blesses us so we can bless others all around the world. God blesses me so I can bless others.

- **How can we show others we think they're very important?**
- **How can we be good friends to others?**
- **How can we say nice things about someone else?**
- **How can we help those nice things to happen for them?**

(Direct some of the answers toward the idea that the best way we can bless others is to let them know God, who will really bless them.)

Song

Sing—and repeat until it's learned—the Psalm 67 Song on the Family Activity Guide.

Reinforcement

Say **God blesses me so I can bless others like Lori. God blesses me so I can bless others like Michael. Say it with me: God blesses me so I can bless others like** (Point to a child and all shout her or his name. Repeat.)

Hold up a stick puppet a child made during the earlier Bible Learn-

ing Activity time. Say, **Here's a girl we'll call Bata from a country called Mongolia on the other side of the world. God blesses me so I can bless others like Bata. How can we bless Bata?** (Be as repetitious as you like to implant the idea that all the steps of blessing can be fulfilled even in a person on the other side of the globe *through our prayers.*) **Here's a boy from Libya we'll call Zamed. God blesses me so I can bless others like Zamed.** (Repeat with other stick puppets.)

Prayer

Thank God that He blesses us to be a blessing to all the peoples of the world.

RELAXING TIME (10-15 MINUTES)

Take children to the restroom a few at a time while other children sing songs, work with skill toys or help prepare snack supplies. Be sure each child as well as teacher washes her or his hands.

SNACKS AND SKIT

Skit Preparation

If you have a large group, divide them into five smaller groups and dress a representative of each group with the following. If a small class, dress each child in one of the following costumes:

- Put big shoes (provided by teachers) over their shoes;
- Decorate their cheeks with stick-on stars or washable spots;
- Dress them in outlandish clothing—loud shirts, funny hats, etc.;
- Dress them in ripped clothing;

Direct children to sit on the floor.

Skit

Dress in a white robe or sheet and tell the children you'll pretend you're Jesus. Have your coactor bring a tray of snacks. As you begin to serve the first group from the tray, tell them not to eat till after you pray.

Your coactor says **Oh, Jesus, don't give them these blessings** (the snacks). **They have such big feet!**

You answer **That doesn't matter. I want to bless all the people of the world.**

Oh, Jesus, don't give them these blessings. They have funny-looking faces.

Again you answer **That doesn't matter. I want to bless all the people of the world.** And so on through your coactor's complaints that they have funny clothes, that they're too poor, etc.

Emphasize that Jesus loves all the people of the world. Then pray, thanking Him for the snacks and for loving all of us.

4s & 5s

TOGETHER FOR SONGS AND FUN (10-15 MINUTES)

Choose from the following options:

Stretching Time

Some children who God wants to bless live far, far away in the world. Let's take a trip and visit them. Lead the children around the world. Climb high mountains, sit in rows on the floor to fly in airplanes, squish together in buses, etc. Stop to stretch out and sleep at night, eat funny food and, most important, meet some of the stick puppet figures who are the children of the world.

Songs

Sing the "Psalm 67 Song" and other favorite songs—especially action songs. (See song suggestions in the Children for the World Bible Learning Activity at the beginning of the lesson plan.)

Bible Learning Activities

Feel free according to your schedule to offer again the activities offered earlier:

- Houses for the World;
- Book Corner;
- All the Children of the World.

Bible Review

Have a few magazines with faces of other cultures available or have several of the houses with faces in the windows from the earlier Bible Learning Activity of Houses for the World. Hold the Bible open to Psalm 67. Say **God blesses me so I can bless others. Does that mean I bless just you, Jason? Just you, Zena? No, God blesses me so I can bless others like this person** (Point to magazine photo of a face.) **and this person. Who is someone you can bless?** (Coach child to answer in frame of "God blesses me so I can bless others like _____.") Close review time in prayer.

Pass out each child's handwork, Student Worksheet and a Family Activity Guide as she or he leaves.

PARTNERS AND PEOPLES

KEY VERSE

"I will bless you,…. And in you all the families of
the earth shall be blessed."
Genesis 12:2,3

KEY BIBLE PASSAGES

Genesis 1:28; 9:1,7; 10:32; 12:2,3; 18:18; 22:17,18; 26:4; 28:14; Psalm
33:12; 46:10; 67:1-4,7; 96:3; Acts 17:27; Luke 24:47; 1 Corinthians 3:9;
Galatians 3:29; Revelation 5:9

OVERVIEW

God has chosen to partner with His people. The partnership works as
He blesses us and we pass on His blessing to the whole world.

AIMS

As a result of this session, your children in Grades 1-3 will:

- Know that we can be partners with God and with each other
  in God's worldwide plan.
- Feel special that God chooses to partner with us.
- Act out in prayer a blessing on one of the world's peoples.

LESSON COMMENTARY

Don't even think about trying to share all this information with your
students. This is background commentary for you as you prepare.

There seems to be more and more nationalistic fervor and ethnic
awareness in our world. And that's only natural—at least since the tower
of Babel! Since God "made from one, every nation [*ethne* in the original
Greek] of mankind to live on the face of the earth, having determined
their appointed times and the boundaries of their habitation" (Acts
17:26). Why did He break up humans into these units? "That they
should seek God, if perhaps they might grope for Him and find Him"
(Acts 17:27). God knows what He's doing on a global scale. Do we?

PEOPLE-GROUP THINKING

In the West, we're usually taught that mankind is divided into geographical, political countries. The Bible, however, describes the world
as divided into cultural groups, families, ethnic and language groups or
nations. As they grow up in the twenty-first century, your students can

grasp this crucial concept: God deals with individuals within groups—people groups.

- Adam and Eve had been told by God to "be fruitful and multiply, and fill the earth" (Genesis 1:28). Then Noah and his sons were twice given that same command: "Be fruitful and multiply, and fill the earth" (Genesis 9:1,7). Why would God want humankind to scatter across the face of the earth? Many Bible scholars feel that a distancing of groups of humans would, first, mean less likelihood of full-scale rebellion and, second, give God more diverse glory. (See Revelation 21:23-26 as the nations bring their glory into the New Jerusalem at the end of time.)
- Humans refused to scatter abroad, and instead built a symbol of their rebellion: the Tower of Babel.

In Genesis 10, humanity had 70 family groupings—which later made up the first nations when their languages were confused: "These are the families of the sons of Noah, according to their genealogies, by their nations; and out of these the nations were separated on the earth after the flood" (Genesis 10:32).

- God told Abraham that He would bless him, and that he and his descendants were to bless these families, nations or peoples of the world. (See Genesis 12:1-3; 18:18; 22:17,18; 26:4; 28:14.) This was a fantastic covenant or partnership God established: He would bless and His people would pass on His offer of blessing to every people.

Abraham's descendants are not just the Jews, not just the God-man Jesus Christ, but also we who belong to Christ: "If you belong to Christ, then you are Abraham's offspring, heirs according to promise" (Galatians 3:29). We too are to "tell of His glory among the nations, His wonderful deeds among *all the peoples*" (Psalm 96:3, italics added). We are to proclaim "repentance for forgiveness of sins…in His name to all the nations" (Luke 24:47).

Your children need to think of the world not in terms of political countries but of people groups.

BLESSED TO BLESS THE PEOPLES

God pours His blessing—His salvation, His presence, His gifts, etc.—into us as His people. But these privileges aren't designed to simply make our own lives nicer. Our earthly role is to be blessed by God and to pass the offer of that blessing of redemption in Christ to every nation—our own included!

- The pattern is summarized in Psalm 67:1,2:

"God be gracious to us and bless us,

And cause His face to shine upon us –

That Thy way may be known on the earth,

Thy salvation among all nations."

We are to:

"Let the people praise Thee, O God;

Let all the peoples praise Thee.

Let the nations be glad and sing for joy" (vv. 3,4).

"God blesses us,

That all the ends of the earth may fear Him" (v. 7).

Some translations of Psalm 67:7 use the conjunction *and* between the clauses. A better translation is *that* because the verse repeats the cause-and-effect sense of the song's beginning: The reason God blesses us on earth is *so that* the people groups of the earth might know His salvation, might know that "blessed is the nation whose God is the Lord" (Psalm 33:12).

- Isn't it amazing—some would say risky—that God chooses to partner with us in order to bless the nations. And isn't it time we recognize that all of us true believers together are in partnership to pass on God's blessing to all the earth's peoples? In the original Greek of the New Testament, the Apostle Paul writes that "We are God's *sunergos*" (1 Corinthians 3:9)—the word from which we get the English term *synergy*. Synergy is a bonding in which the sum is greater than the individual parts. That's the Body of Christ worldwide: *God's synergy*.

- *All* the nations will be blessed. That is, every distinct group of people will be offered the blessing of God. And in every people group, some will respond. The Apostle John saw in the future that some representatives of every nation are gathered around the throne of the Lamb: some "from every tribe and tongue and people and nation" (Revelation 5:9).

All the nations includes our own people, of course. So all of us believers in Jesus Christ have some blessing to do—among our own people and/or to other people groups.

If the Lord allows it, the children in your class will be facing a brave new world in their futures. The fact that we're blessed to bless the nations as we partner with God and each other will help prepare your students for that world and their parts in it. They'll be much more up-to-speed than many of us whose constant cry is only the "Bless me" part of God's historic plan!

PERSONAL POP QUIZ

It's one thing to rattle through a lesson about God's great, global purpose. It's another thing to look in the mirror and ask yourself as a children's worker some serious questions:

- Do I recognize every blessing in my life as having a distinct purpose in others' lives in every nation?

- Can I quote the remainder of "Be still, and…" (Psalm 46:10, *NIV*) or am I perhaps a bit focused on myself and what blessings I can get out of God? (Go ahead and check the reference.) Am I as a partner going about the Father's business or am I designing my own plans?

- Do I really think it's possible that these children I'm teaching will be guiding the global vision of the church in the twenty-first century? Or is that one of the reasons I plead with Jesus to return *soon*?

For Further Personal Study

- Read through the globe-trotting Bible study *Catch the Vision 2000* by Bill and Amy Stearns (Bethany House). Available at Christian bookstores or call 800-MISSION.

For Further Mission Vision Materials for Children

- *The Great KidMission;* Gospel Light Publications, 2300 Knoll Dr., Ventura, CA 93003; Phone: 800-446-7735; Fax: 800-860-3109. This resource is a compendium of ideas and resources for involving children in active learning about missions around the world. The book contains a great variety of resources to meet the needs of those who want to create a customized five- to ten-day Children's Missions Conference, extend Vacation Bible School or enrich Kids' Club and Sunday School programs.

- Contact Kids Can Make A Difference, 4445 Webster Drive, York, PA 17402; Phone: 800-543-7554. Request a KidsCan Network Catalog with its up-to-date listing of mission resources for children. To join a computer network of adults who work with children's mission materials and ideas, find someone in your fellowship with a computer and a modem. Have her or him subscribe to this free network for you. Send an e-mail message to:

  kidscan@xc.org

  Leave the "subject" area blank or hit the space bar. Put in the message area: *Subscribe kids-can-net* and add your e-mail address. You'll automatically begin receiving information on networking and on the best mission materials for children.

LESSON PLAN

Note: Much of the following material was adapted from lessons by Jan Bell, founder of KidsCan. (See above for contact information.)

PREPARATION

1. Study the Bible passages listed and the material in your Lesson Commentary.
2. Pray that God will help your students catch the idea that God wants to use them in His great plans.
3. Think through the following Lesson Plan activities.
4. Prepare materials as listed in the box.

MATERIALS NEEDED

- A Bible for each student;
- A photocopy of the Student Worksheet for each expected student and visitor;
- A ball of yarn or string for one of the opening activities;

- A photocopy of the Family Activity Guide for each student;
- A globe—preferably an inflatable or sponge type, or an inflated balloon with continents outlined with a felt-tip pen, or a world map will suffice (optional);
- A world map cut up in 20-30 pieces to make a puzzle and transparent tape (optional for the Alternate Focus Bible Learning Activity);
- A few pieces of old and odd clothes, two or three stickers, a sheet, robe or sign that says "Jesus" and snacks (optional for Decide snack skit).

SESSION AT A GLANCE

Opening Activities

Focus (5 Minutes)

Story: "Called on the Carpet"

(Alternate Focus Bible Learning Activity: The Put-Your-World-Together Puzzle)

Discover (12-15 Minutes)

Bible Study Word Games

Key Verse Memorization

Decide (15 Minutes)

The Worldwide Wish List

(Alternate Decide activities: Games, songs and a snacks skit)

Do (2-3 Minutes)

Middle-Eastern-Style Prayer

(Alternate Do Bible Learning Activity: The Psalm 67 Song)

THE SESSION

OPENING ACTIVITIES

Use this time when students arrive as you normally do:
- Greet each student by name. Make an effort to comment on, ask a question of, sit down with or in some way connect personally with each student. Ask **Did you know this is *A Sunday for the World*?**
- Take care of attendance and visitor information business.
- Invite students into active involvement as they arrive. Consider the following activities. These may be used later or even used again during the session:

Partners

Children sit back-to-back with a partner on the floor, knees bent with feet on the floor. Arms are crossed in front of them. When you give the signal, the pairs try to stand up without using their hands. They'll dis-

Note: This Partners Around the World activity can be easily expanded as a learning activity. The string or yarn used can be red to symbolize the bond true Christians worldwide have through the blood of Jesus. Children can cut out magazine pictures of foreign faces from mission magazines, *National Geographic* magazine, etc. These pictures, mounted on construction paper, can be hung by a string around each child's neck.

An alternate approach is to attach a name tag to each child. The name tag has the name of a people group in the world which has a strong church movement of its own—people groups such as the Mexican, German, Javanese (in Indonesia), Russian, Han (Chinese), Australian, Swedish, Argentinean, Scottish, Cherokee, Korean, Samoan, etc., peoples. These are people groups whose churches we need to partner with. But there are unreached peoples in the world, too. You can make a show of producing several name tags that list unreached people groups—those cultures that don't have a church we can partner with. These groups aren't part of our circle yet—people groups such as the Turkmen (see story below), the Kurds of Iraq or the people group actually called the Bozos of Mali in West Africa. You can stop to pray for these unreached peoples who aren't yet part of our partnership with God because they haven't yet heard about Jesus.

cover it's difficult to stand simply by pushing back-to-back. Allow the pairs several attempts. Then tell them to hook elbows as they sit back-to-back. At your signal, they again try to stand and find that it's far easier when they are linked with one another. Point out that when we are linked firmly with God, when we partner with Him, things happen.

Three-Legged Race

Pair children with a partner side-by-side and tie their center legs together with strips of cloth. Then, according to your setting, race sets of partners or simply time a pair of partners as they navigate from one end of the room to the other. Point out that if we work together with our partners, we can cover some ground. If we don't cooperate with our partners, we usually fall flat on our faces.

Partners Around the World

Join the children seated in a circle on the floor. Hold a ball of yarn or string and explain that all around the world are Christians with whom we can partner. Ask what the children see in the middle of the circle now. (Nothing.) Say **Now watch what happens when one person who loves Jesus partners with another.** Then hold the end of the yarn or string and toss it to a child across the circle. That child holds the yarn at that point and tosses it to another child until each has been connected with another believer. Say **Look at what a beautiful pattern the yarn makes when we partner with each other around the world.**

Direct the children to carefully stand while still holding the yarn tightly. Carefully choose a child or two to pull (not yank) harder in his or her direction. What happens? The design is distorted. Point out that if we think we're the only ones, we might pull too hard and the partnership of Christians around the world doesn't look too good.

Now demonstrate what happens when we don't hold onto our links with other Christians around the world. Have one or two children let go of the yarn. Ask, **What happens to the design and shape of our world when we let go of our part in the partnership? Today we'll be learning about partnering with God and partnering with all God's people around the world.**

GATHERING ACTIVITIES

As the children gather for the lesson, use the following activities to help them begin thinking about partnering with God:

Ask **Sometimes you need someone else to do something such as play soccer or tell jokes. What are other things you like to do that need more than just you?** Let the children brainstorm and tell their stories.

Say **The different parts of our body work together. What if the rest of the body said, "We don't need those legs." Try to crawl without using your legs.**

What if the rest of the body said, "We don't need fingers." Try to write with this pencil without using your fingers.

What if the rest of the body said, "We don't need the tongue." Touch your tongue to the inside of your cheek and say your name and where you go to school.

Try learning the song "God Wants to Partner with Us" or the "Psalm 67 Song" (on the Family Activity Guide).

FOCUS (5 MINUTES)

This segment is designed to interest your students in the theme of the lesson.

Story: "Called on the Carpet"

Gather your students for a story. ("Called on the Carpet" is fictional.) Tell them this is *A Sunday for the World*. Present the story from memory or read it with dramatic flair. If you have a globe or world map, point out the setting of the story, the new country of Turkmenistan, one of the former Soviet republics on the southeast corner of the Caspian Sea. (Don't linger, squinting at the map as if it will make any difference to your children *exactly* where Turkmenistan is.) The people here are the Turkmen (not the Turks of Turkey). Most of the country is desert, and except in the cities the people live in huge tents called *yurts*. There are no known Turkmen churches.

Called on the Carpet

By Ginny Williams

The dark interior of the domed sheepskin yurt blinded Awazed as he entered from the blazing desert sunlight. As he walked down the smoke-blackened hall to the cooking fire, the chatting and laughter of his female relatives—grandmother, mother, aunts and cousins—drew him further.

"Grandfather has been asking for you," his elder sister said as Awazed handed her the lamb and rice he had just purchased at the open air market. "He has more work for you to do before the honored guest arrives."

"I will go to him at once," Awazed replied. It was difficult not to be nervous, as he entered the male quarters and went quickly to Grandfather's side. As he kissed Grandfather's hand and bowed low to place it on his own forehead, Grandfather spoke.

"Awazed, my son, I trust that all of the necessary preparations are being made?"

"Yes, Grandfather, I am your slave," Awazed replied.

"Good. Sweep the carpet and arrange the cushions. Our guest will be arriving within the half hour."

"Yes, Grandfather, I will at once!" Awazed quickly began sweeping the large family carpet with a makeshift broom. The intricate pattern of deep crimson, cream, bright green and dark brown that had belonged to his family throughout the generations held his attention as he listened to the conversation surrounding him. "Father, this Western guest," his uncle mused, "How does he come to visit us? The villagers say that he speaks with great wisdom, yet of unusual things about his God."

"Are we not the craftsmen of the most beautiful carpets in all of Turkmenia?" Grandfather inquired.

"Yes, our father," came the joint reply.

"Well, then, why shouldn't the first Westerner to enter our village be shown the hospitality of the most illustrious clan?" Grandfather asked. "While at the carpet bazaar, this man commented on the beauty and quality of our women's handwork. Your eldest brother, of course, invited him for a feast. I honor you, my son, for your wisdom." Grandfather nodded toward Awazed's father as he paid him this deep compliment. Such a feast was a great expense and sacrifice for the family, an unusual departure from the daily bread, rice and tea.

"It is my honor, Father," he replied. "For your honor," Grandfather continued, "I give to your eldest son, Awazed, the pleasure of serving tea to our guest."

Astonished, Awazed lifted his head to speak, but caught himself in time and returned to his work.

"Awazed, how do you reply?" his father inquired.

"I am deeply honored, my grandfather. In my serving, I will honor you," Awazed replied. His head swimming, Awazed was dismissed to make the necessary preparations for *chai*—the tea. Shortly, the tent buzzed with word of the guest's arrival. Peering through the roughened flaps of the yurt, Awazed caught a glimpse of a fair-skinned man with glistening red hair. How odd he looked among all of his dark-haired relatives. *What are the unusual things he has to say about God?* he wondered. Before his thoughts could carry him further, Awazed saw his relatives leading the guest indoors. He wiped the sweat from his hands and hurried to the fire. Anxiously, he rehearsed serving *chai* to the guest over and over in his head. "I mustn't disappoint Grandfather. I must do this right or we will be disgraced," Awazed told himself as he arranged the porcelain tea service on the black lacquered tray.

Pulling himself erect, Awazed took a deep breath as he entered the men's quarters, keeping a careful eye on the tray. Proudly, his father directed him toward the guest. "Mr. Groves, I present to you, my eldest son, Awazed." As Awazed looked up, his foot caught the fringed edge of the carpet and he tumbled to the floor. The clatter of smashing cups filled Awazed's ears as he landed face down on the prized family carpet. He heard the intake of breath in chorus from the circle around him and Awazed moaned as he awaited certain reprimand. Silence hung in the air. For Awazed, eternity passed in seconds. He braced himself for the outburst.

Suddenly, an explosion of sound rolled over Awazed. It was laughter! Looking up, he saw the honored guest laughing heartily. Awazed cautiously looked at the other faces surrounding him and watched as their expressions of horror were replaced by puzzlement. Slowly, a smile crossed Grandfather's face as he began to chuckle, the rest of the room joining in. Confused, Awazed stared. "Awazed," the guest called out between chuckles, "come sit by me on the carpet. I have something to tell you." Awazed glanced at Grandfather. After a quick nod, he knew he must obey. But how could he take the place of highest honor after such a disgrace?

Bewildered, he complied and listened intently as the guest continued. "There is a story in our holy book, the Bible. In the story, a young boy leaves his father's home with a portion of his father's

70

estate before he is of age." Everyone in the room nodded knowingly, for the Turkmen do not leave their father's home with their portion until the age of forty. "He takes his father's wealth and spends it on many pleasures until, one day, his money is gone. His friends desert him and he wanders looking for work in order to buy food. However, there is no work except to tend the pigs of a foreign landowner."

Awazed cringed as he imagined this disgrace. He would never think of touching a pig! To the Turkmen, who call themselves Muslims, working with pigs or eating the meat of pigs is disgusting!

"Finally," the guest said, "the son thinks to himself, 'Even the lowest in my father's house are better off than this. I will return home and ask to be treated as a hired servant.' So the young man goes home, expecting the worst. Instead, his father runs to greet him, kisses him, gives him his own ring and places a beautiful coat upon him. He gives a party to celebrate his son's return! Even after disgracing his father, this son was forgiven and given the highest honor. With your grandfather's permission, I forgive you and ask you to sit with me for the meal."

Amazed, Awazed looked to Grandfather, who nodded his approval. Awazed beamed as he settled next to the guest on the carpet. He did not fully understand this new idea, forgiveness, but he was certain he wanted to know more.

Opening Prayer

Thank God that His forgiving relationship with us allows us to have relationships with people all across the world—people like the Turkmen. Pray that this *A Sunday for the World* session will help us partner with God and His people to reach groups like the Turkmen.

ALTERNATE FOCUS BIBLE LEARNING ACTIVITY (5 MINUTES)

Put Your World Together (5 Minutes)

Distribute to each student two or three pieces of the world map puzzle you have previously cut up. Clear a space on the floor and set out the tape. Tell the class this is *A Sunday for the World*. Challenge them on how quickly they can fit and tape the pieces together into a world map. Once completed, hang the map—regardless of its probably haggard appearance—on a wall or bulletin board for reference during the session. As you hang the map, point out that it took teamwork to put the world map together. Say **Today we'll see how all of us believers in Jesus are partners in what God is doing in the world.** Open your *A Sunday for the World* session in prayer.

DISCOVER (12-15 MINUTES)

These activities get your students into the Bible to discover what God says about His partnership with us.

Bible Study Word Games (8-10 Minutes)

Pass out Student Worksheets and allow about four to five minutes for students to complete.

Look up the Bible references together and let the children compare answers. Comment on students' answers from your own study and from information in the Lesson Commentary.

Say **As we partner together with God, He blesses us to bless every people in the world. Every people will be a part of God's family since there will be some from every people around the throne of the Lamb. So it's only a matter of when and of who will partner with God to do it.**

Maybe some in your class will bring the gospel to one of the world's remaining unreached peoples.

Answers:

The Theme for *A Sunday for the World*

Fill in the blanks: God said, "I will _____bless_____ you and you will be a _____blessing_____ to all the _____peoples_____."

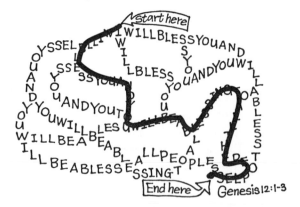

Partnering with God

Fill in the missing vowels—a, e, i, o, u—for the answer.

That His w<u>a</u>y m<u>a</u>y b<u>e</u> kn<u>o</u>wn <u>a</u>m<u>o</u>ng <u>a</u>ll n<u>a</u>ti<u>o</u>ns, His s<u>a</u>lv<u>a</u>ti<u>o</u>n <u>a</u>m<u>o</u>ng <u>a</u>ll p<u>eo</u>ples.

Partners in Heaven

Key Verse Memorization (4-5 Minutes)

Use the tried-and-true method of group memorization below—or your own favorite method—to help students learn:

"I will bless you,... And in you all the families of the earth shall be blessed" (Genesis 12:2,3).

- Write the verse including the reference on the board or flipchart as you say the words together.
- Mention that seven is thought of as the perfect number in the Bible. So read the verse together seven times.
- Erase or black out two words and together repeat the verse. Repeat this process—sometimes having an individual repeat the verse after you've erased another word or two—until all the words are erased.
- Ask for volunteers to recite the verse.
- Have everyone turn over their Student Worksheets and try to write out the verse.

Conclude this activity with lots of praise and a reminder that the verse is talking about our worldwide partnership with God: He blesses us so that we will be a blessing to all the world's peoples.

DECIDE (6-8 MINUTES)
This segment of the lesson helps children start seeing the applications of our global partnership with God and with His people.

The Worldwide Wish List (6-8 Minutes)
Write on the board or flipchart "If I could do anything to change the world, I would…." Say **Let's see why it is so important to partner together to be a blessing to all the world's peoples. How would each of you end this phrase?** Give a few ideas first. Then ask each child for a response. Jot key words of these responses on the board or flipchart. Expect simple, repeated wishes: peace, food for the hungry, etc.

Ask **Why are there such problems in the world? Is it because God doesn't love people?** No. Sometimes it's because of Satan. Sometimes because of what sin has done to the world. Very often it's because God's people—the true Christians of the world—aren't partnering with God and with each other to make a difference in the world.

Here's an example of a child who partnered to make a difference. Read the following:

Hope Smith was eleven years old when she was required to do a school report on the people of Mongolia. She says, "I was fascinated by the land of Genghis Khan, a nation where nomads live in beautiful felt tents made from sheep wool. Inside these tents are colorful felt coverings, lovely carved chests—even TVs and radios. Unfortunately, there are also Bhuddist altars in there. When the paper was almost finished, I came across an article in our church's magazine about how few Christians there were in Mongolia. Reading that article shocked me into praying every day."

Hope found out about the few Christians in Mongolia from her church's mission magazine—one of the partners God works through. And so she began to pray, "Lord, please help the people in Mongolia, and replace those Buddhist altars in their felt tents with Bibles." Hope prayed this prayer for two years!

She says, "Last month in the magazine rack at church I saw another issue of the mission agency magazine. What caught my eye was the bold title on the front of the magazine: 'Hope for Mongo-

lia.' Now, my name is Hope, but they weren't talking about me. They were talking about a week-long crusade where 500 Mongolians responded to the gospel! Little did they know when they wrote those words that there is another Hope for Mongolia—and that Hope is me!"

Point out that Hope was partnering with God and with her church's mission agency to pray not once or twice but for two years for Mongolia. Take your globe, balloon with the continents drawn in or a world map. Have a child point out your location and the location of Mongolia (between Russia and China). Suggest that we, like Hope, can partner with God to change things even on the other side of the world.

Refer to the Worldwide Wish List "If I could do anything..." and the responses you jotted on the board or flipchart. Encourage students to think what might happen if we changed the "I" in the "I would..." to "God and I and all the true Christians in the whole world."

Consider handing the globe, balloon or map to each child and asking her or him to pray for the world according to their Worldwide Wish List wish. Give examples of your own prayers: **Lord, I want to partner with you to feed hungry children in Africa. Lord, help Christians to partner together and spread the gospel in Mongolia.** Offer to pray the wish of any children too shy to pray aloud.

Action Games, Songs and/or Snacks (7-9 Minutes)

Choose any of the following reinforcement activities as your time and students' attention spans permit. Initiate or repeat some of the action games listed above under Opening Activities. Consider using some of the following activities as well:

- Drawing: Children draw themselves among the group of children on the Partners Across the World segment of their Student Worksheets.
- Game: Play the Prui Game. (You can choose any foreign-sounding name.) Explain the game: **You will all be blind (your eyes closed) except one person who will be Prui. I'll pick that person just before we start the game. When you bump into someone, you must ask, "Prui?" They must answer, "Prui?" If someone bumps into you, you must also say, "Prui?" If the person you bump into says nothing, then you have found Prui, and you can open your eyes and hold hands. Then you both are Prui and say nothing when someone bumps into you. Then she can open her eyes and join hands with you and so on. Let's try it.**

Have everyone stand in a central play area with eyes closed. Whisper into several children's ears **You are not Prui.** Whisper in one child's ear **You are Prui. You can open your eyes but you cannot speak.** At your signal, the children move about with eyes still closed. When they bump into someone, they ask and answer, "Prui?" Remind them that Prui will not say anything, so if they bump into someone who doesn't ask, "Prui?" they may open their eyes and join hands. Prui will grow a line, of course, with children joining hands at either end where there are hands to be held. Once everyone has found Prui and has joined hands, have all join hands into a circle.

74

Point out to the circle that everyone in the world once walked in spiritual blindness until our eyes are opened by the light of the gospel. We then have partnership with God and with His growing Body of Christians across the world. We need to keep seeking those whose eyes are still closed to the light of the gospel until they have a partnership with God and with us, too.

- 10/40 Window Map: Especially if your fellowship has had an emphasis on praying for the peoples of the 10/40 Window, pause to reinforce the importance of this area of the world:

Say **Look on your Student Worksheet world map. Draw a line from the bulge of West Africa across the middle of the Philippine Islands. That's the ten degree north latitude—the lines maps use for locating places. Draw another line from Spain across to Japan. That's the forty degree north latitude. Now box in the ends. This is the world's "10/40 Window." It has the poorest of the world's poor. And most of the world's unreached peoples are in this box. Let's pray now for God to break through with His love to these people groups, and for more Christians to partner together to reach the 10/40 Window with the gospel.**

- Song: With younger children, learn and sing the song "God Wants to Partner with Us" to the tune of "Pop Goes the Weasel." Begin by standing in a circle.

God wants to partner with us; (Move in one

    direction.)

A faithful Friend is He. (Move in opposite

    direction.)

We work together to spread the Good News.

(Hunch down on heels as if planting seeds.)

And set the captives free! (Jump up, arms

    upraised.)

(Adapted from lyrics by Margie Marsh of KidsCan Associates.)

- Song: Learn and sing "Psalm 67 Song" (on the Family Activity Guide each child will take home).
- Snack and Skit: With younger children, consider presenting a special snack and skit. You'll need an assistant to serve the snacks as your coactor.

Skit Preparation:

- Outfit each child in one of the following costumes:
  — Put big shoes (provided by you and your coworker) on their feet;
  — Have them slip on some kind of outlandish clothing—loud shirts, funny hats, etc.;
  — Have them slip on some kind of ripped clothing;
  — Tell one or two children who don't want to be costumed to talk softly in made-up words as if speaking a foreign language;
  — Put stickers on their foreheads or cheeks.

Skit:

Wrap yourself in a sheet or a white robe—or wear a sign that says, "Jesus"—and tell the children you'll pretend you're Jesus. Have your coworker bring a tray of snacks. As you begin to serve the first child or group from the tray, tell them not to eat till after you pray.

Your coactor says **Oh, Jesus, don't give them snacks. They have really big feet!**

You answer **That doesn't matter. I love all the people of the world.**

Oh, Jesus, don't give them snacks. They have funny-looking faces.

Again you answer **That doesn't matter. I love all the people of the world.** And so on through your coactor's complaints that they have funny clothes, that they're too poor, that they speak with funny words, etc.

Emphasize that Jesus loves all the people of the world—even the ones very different from us. Then pray, asking His blessing on the snack and on us to be blessings to all the different people in the world.

DO (2-3 MINUTES)

This segment of your lesson is designed to help students reinforce through action what they've learned.

Prayers for the Peoples

Say **In many parts of the world, believers don't close their eyes and bow their heads to pray. Often they keep their eyes open and look upward. Let's try that. Stand and pray silently along with me as I pray.**

In your prayer, praise the Lord that He blesses us and lets us partner with Him and each other to change the world. Thank Him for blessings such as prayer, and feel free to bless the nations yourself by praying for a people group or two—our own included.

Make sure each student has a Family Activity Guide.

ALTERNATE DO BIBLE LEARNING ACTIVITY (2-3 MINUTES)

Choose this activity if you have more time.

Blessed to Be a Blessing Song

Repeat the "Psalm 67 Song" on the Family Activity Guide until your class learns it from memory. Then in the three beats following each "all the peoples of the world," have students take turns calling out, "like _____" (a people group). Hopefully you'll be hearing the names of some of the people groups mentioned during the lesson: "like Mongolians! like the Turkmen! like the Russians!"

Be sure each student has a Family Activity Guide to take home after you close in prayer.

STUDENT WORKSHEET

THE THEME FOR *A SUNDAY FOR THE WORLD*

1. Look up Genesis 12:1-3. Fill in the blanks: God said, "I will _____ you and you will be a _____ to all the _____."

2. Trace a line through the correct order of letters from the "I" to the "Genesis 12:1-3" reference.

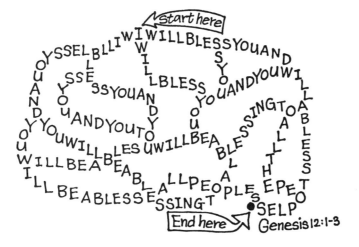

PARTNERING WITH GOD

When we partner with God, He blesses us. Why?

Fill in the missing vowels—a, e, i, o, u—for the answer.

That His w_y m_y b_ kn_wn _m_ng _ll n_t_ _ ns, His s_lv_t_ _ n _m_ng _ll p__pl_s.

Look up Psalm 67:1,2 to check your answer.

PARTNERS IN HEAVEN

Partnering with God and the hundreds of millions of other Christians around the world means inviting boys, girls, men and women to heaven. Who will be in heaven?

Fill in the columns in alphabetical order to find out. (Example: The first blank needs an *s* to follow *q* and *r*. The second blank needs the letter that comes between *n* and *p*, and so on.

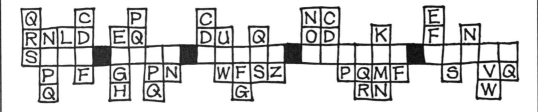

Look up Revelation 5:9 to check your answer.

PARTNERS AROUND THE WORLD—INCLUDING YOU

Draw yourself among these other followers of Jesus from around the world.

PRIESTS FOR THE PEOPLES

KEY VERSE

"God blesses us, that all the ends of the earth may fear Him." Psalm 67:7

KEY BIBLE PASSAGES

Genesis 1:28; 2:1-3; 9:1,7; 22:17,18; 26:4; 28:14; Exodus 19:5,6; Psalm 33:12; 67:1-4,7; 87:6; 96:3; Malachi 1:11; Matthew 28:19; Luke 24:47; Acts 17:26, 27; Galatians 3:29; 1 Peter 2:9, 10; Revelation 5:9

OVERVIEW

God's people are a nation of priests. And priests have a job to do—interceding for and ministering to the peoples of the world.

AIMS

As a result of this session, your children in Grades 4-6 will:

- Know that humankind is a mosaic of different peoples, each of which is special in God's eyes.
- Feel important as a priest—one who is blessed in order to bless every people.
- Act out in prayer a priestly blessing on one of the planet's people groups.

LESSON COMMENTARY

Don't even think about trying to share all this information with your students. This is background commentary for you as you prepare.

There seems to be more and more nationalistic fervor and ethnic awareness in our world. And that's only natural—at least since the tower of Babel!—since God "made from one, every nation [*ethne* in the original Greek] of mankind to live on the face of the earth, having determined their appointed times and the boundaries of their habitation" (Acts 17:26). Why did He break up humans into these units? "That they should seek God, if perhaps they might grope for Him and find Him" Acts 17:27). God knows what He's doing. Do we?

PEOPLE-GROUP THINKING

In the West, we're usually taught that mankind is divided into geographical, political countries. The Bible, however, describes the world as divided into cultural groups, families, ethnic and language groups or nations. As they grow up in the twenty-first century, your students can grasp this crucial concept: God deals with individuals within groups—people groups.

- Adam and Eve had been told by God to "be fruitful and multiply, and fill the earth" (Genesis 1:28). Then Noah and his sons were twice given that same command: "Be fruitful and multiply, and fill the earth" (Genesis 9:1,7). Why would God want humankind to scatter across the face of the earth? Many Bible scholars feel that a distancing of groups of humans would first mean less likelihood of full-scale rebellion and second, give God more diverse glory. (See Revelation 21:23-26 as the nations bring their glory into the New Jerusalem at the end of time.)

- Humans refused to scatter abroad, and instead built a symbol of their rebellion: the Tower of Babel.

   In Genesis 10, humanity had 70 family groupings—which later made up the first nations when their languages were confused: "These are the families of the sons of Noah, according to their genealogies, by their nations, and out of these the nations were separated on the earth after the flood" (Genesis 10:32).

- God told Abraham that He would bless him, and that he and his descendants were to bless these families, nations or peoples of the world. (See Genesis 12:1-3; 18:18; 22:17,18; 26:4; 28:14.) This was a fantastic covenant or partnership God established: He would bless and His people would pass on His offer of blessing to every people.

   Abraham's descendants are not just the Jews, not just the God-man Jesus Christ, but also we who belong to Christ: "If you belong to Christ, then you are Abraham's offspring, heirs according to promise" (Galatians 3:29). We too are to "tell of His glory among the nations, His wonderful deeds among *all the peoples*" (Psalm 96:3, italics added). We are commanded to make disciples of *all nations (ethne)*" (Matthew 28:19, italics added). We are to proclaim "repentance for forgiveness of sins in His name to *all the nations*" (Luke 24:47, italics added).

   Your children need to think of the world not in terms of political countries but of people groups.

BLESSED TO BLESS THE PEOPLES

God pours His blessing—His salvation, His presence, His gifts, etc.—into us as His people. But these privileges aren't designed to simply make our own lives nicer. Our earthly role is to be blessed by God and to pass the offer of that blessing of redemption in Christ to every nation—our own included!

- The pattern is summarized in Psalm 67:1,2:

"God be gracious to us and bless us,
And cause His face to shine upon us—
That Thy way may be known on the earth,
Thy salvation among all nations."

We are to:

"Let the peoples praise Thee, O God;

Let all the peoples praise Thee.

Let the nations be glad and sing for joy" (vv. 3,4).

"God blesses us,

That all the ends of the earth may fear Him" (v. 7).

Some translations of Psalm 67:7 use the conjunction *and* between the clauses. A better translation is *that* because the verse repeats the cause-and-effect sense of the song's beginning: The reason God blesses us on earth is *so that* the people groups of the earth might know His salvation, might know that "blessed is the nation whose God is the Lord" (Psalm 33:12).

A good picture of how God uses us to bless the nations is seen in our role as a nation of priests.

There is great privilege in the priesthood of the believer. But often we stop at that privilege of entering into the presence of God without need of a mediator other than Christ Himself. With privilege comes responsibility. And the responsibility of a priest is first to intercede for the people and second, to serve them. We as a heavenly nation of priests are to be interceding for the earthbound nations of the world—our own ethnic group included. And we are to find our place in serving them in the name of Jesus. (See Exodus 19:5,6 and 1 Peter 2:9,10.)

All the nations will be blessed. That is, every distinct group of people will be offered the blessing of redemption in Jesus Christ. And in every people group, some will respond. The Apostle John saw in the future that some representatives of every nation are gathered around the throne of the Lamb: "some from every tribe and tongue and people and nation" (Revelation 5:9).

God lists even some of Israel's worst enemies as being represented in the heavenly City of Zion—including some Egyptians (symbolized by the name Rahab), Babylonians and Philistines. God is so specific about each group having representatives in heaven that He has a great book called the Register of the Peoples. (See Psalm 87:6.)

Offering His blessing to *all* the nations includes our own people, of course. So all believers in Jesus Christ have some blessing to do—among our own people and/or to other people groups.

If the Lord allows it, your Bible class children will be facing a brave new world in their futures. People-group thinking and the fact that we're blessed to bless the nations are two big-picture concepts that will help prepare your students for that world and their part in it. They'll be much more up-to-speed than many of us political-country-thinkers whose constant cry is only the "Bless me" part of God's historic plan!

PERSONAL POP QUIZ

It's one thing to rattle through a lesson about God's great, global purpose. It's another thing to look in the mirror and ask yourself as a children's worker some serious questions:

- Do I recognize every blessing in my life as having a distinct purpose in others' lives in every nation?
- Can I quote the remainder of "Be still, and..." (Psalm 46:10, *NIV*) or am I perhaps a bit focused on myself and what blessings I can get out of God? (Go ahead and check the reference.)
- Do I really think it's possible these children I'm teaching will be guiding the global vision of the church in the twenty-first century? Or is that one of the reasons I plead with Jesus to return *soon*?

For Further Study

- Read through the globe-trotting Bible study *Catch the Vision 2000* by Bill and Amy Stearns (Bethany House). Available at Christian bookstores or call 800-MISSION.

For Further Mission Vision Materials for Children

- *The Great KidMission;* Gospel Light Publications, 2300 Knoll Dr., Ventura, CA 93003; Phone: 800-446-7735; Fax: 800-860-3109. This resource is a compendium of ideas and resources for involving children in active learning about missions around the world. The book contains a great variety of resources to meet the needs of those who want to create a customized five- to ten-day Children's Missions Conference, extend Vacation Bible School or enrich Kids' Club and Sunday School programs.
- Contact Kids Can Make a Difference, 4445 Webster Drive, York, PA 17402; Phone: 800-543-7554. Request a KidsCan Network Catalog with its up-to-date listing of mission resources for children. To join a computer network of adults who work with children's mission materials and ideas, find someone in your fellowship with a computer and a modem. Have her or him subscribe to this free network for you. Send an e-mail message to:

  kidscan@xc.org

  Leave the "subject" area blank or hit the space bar. Put in the message area: *Subscribe kids-can-net* and add your e-mail address. You'll automatically begin receiving information on networking and on the best mission materials for children.

LESSON PLAN

PREPARATION

1. Study the Bible passages listed and the material in your Lesson Commentary. This material may present a new perspective on God's heart for every people, so study thoroughly.
2. Pray that God will help your students catch a vision of His world and their parts in it.
3. Think through the following Lesson Plan activities. If possible, spend enough time reviewing the "Brazil-Fulani-Hawaii Connection" story (a Focus Bible Learning Activity) to be able to tell it to your class without reading it.

MATERIALS NEEDED

- A Bible for each student;
- A photocopy of the Student Worksheet for each expected student and visitor;
- Scissors, tape, crayons or markers and a large sheet of paper for each student (construction paper, legal-size paper, a piece of butcher paper, etc.);
- A photocopy of the Family Activity Guide for each student;
- Chalkboard, white board or a large piece of butcher paper and enough markers, crayons or chalk for each student (optional for Alternate Focus Bible Learning Activity);
- A globe or world map;
- Photocopies of the "Synchronized Reading Scripts", a tape recorder and cassette tape. If you choose this activity, your class won't need copies of the Student Worksheet (optional for Alternate Discover Bible Learning Activity).

SESSION AT A GLANCE

Opening Activities

Focus (6-8 Minutes)

Story: "The Brazil-Fulani-Hawaii Connection"

(Alternate Focus Bible Learning Activity: A New World Map)

Discover (15-18 Minutes)

Bible Study Word Games: People-Group Thinking

Demonstration: You, A Priest

(Alternate Discover Bible Learning Activity: Blessed to Bless the Peoples—A Synchronized Reading and Taping)

Decide (10-12 Minutes)

The Tower of Babel Prayer Reminder

(Alternate Decide Activities: Compiling Answers and A Mini-Registry of the Peoples)

Do (2-3 Minutes)

Written Prayers for the Peoples

(Alternate Do Bible Learning Activity: The Psalm 67 Song)

THE SESSION

OPENING ACTIVITIES

FOCUS (6-8 MINUTES)

This segment of your lesson hooks students' interests in today's topic.

Story: The Brazil-Fulani
(foo-lah-nee)-Hawaii Connection

Gather your students for a good story. The story is true and took place in 1992.

As you mention places, point out on a globe or world map your own location in relation to Brazil, Guinea-Bissau (bih-*sow*) on the coast of West Africa and Hawaii. Try to tell the story from memory if you can. Even if you read it, remember that eye contact during a dramatic story is crucial. Don't worry about your pronunciation or about remembering every detail. For example, the names of the people involved and other facts are in parentheses for your information, not necessarily for your listeners. Storytelling is for emotional—not intellectual—impact!

The Brazil-Fulani (foo-lah-nee)-Hawaii Connection

Just a few years ago some churches in Brazil sent out one of their missionary teams. Did you know Brazilians send thousands of missionaries now to places all across the world? This team went to the Fulani people of a country called Guinea-Bissau in Africa. The Fulani people have always refused to become Christians. They call themselves Muslims, but they mostly believe in magic and evil spirits, and they hate Christianity! (Muslims believe in Allah and follow very strict but simple religious practices. Most Muslims sincerely want a relationship with God, but don't recognize Jesus as the Way, the Truth and the Life. Only very few Muslims are the fanatical kind we read about in newspaper articles on terrorism.)

The Brazilian missionaries settled in a Fulani village (in Gabu, Guinea-Bissau). They lived in the same kind of huts the Fulani did, and they ate the same food the Fulani ate.

One morning soon after they arrived, one of the Brazilian couples (João and Solange Oliveira) who were expecting a baby got very worried. The baby was coming a month early! And they were miles from the nearest hospital. Just six hours after Baby Rebecca was born, she died.

The husband sadly went to the Bigman, the chief of the village, and asked if he could bury the baby in the village cemetery. The Bigman said, "You are foreigners, but you live as we do. And now you want to become like us and bury your loved one in our Muslim cemetery? Yes, you may. And you may do it in your Christian way."

That afternoon, the Brazilian couple walked slowly behind a Fulani man who carried Baby Rebecca's casket. Behind them winding out from the village were twenty of the area's Muslim leaders, other members of the Brazilian mission team and then hundreds of Fulani villagers. At the cemetery, the team leader said that sometimes God allows a seed to die and be planted in the ground before new life springs forth.

Here's the new life.

Two days later Clarice, a young lady of the Brazilian team, walked an hour and a half through the heat to a neighboring Fulani village (Casambe). When Clarice asked the two Bigmen for permission to tell the people about *Isa*, Jesus the Messiah, they said,

"We know who you are. You are the foreigners who have lived among us. You have buried your baby in our Muslim cemetery. You are one with us now. Let us first send out runners to gather all the people from the fields."

The 150 villagers settled on the ground around Clarice as, through an interpreter, she told the villagers about Jesus Christ. Then she asked who would follow *Isa*. Fifty-four Fulani stood, including the two Bigmen.

Clarice widened her eyes. Maybe they misunderstood her message. She motioned for everyone to sit down again. A second time she explained the gospel and the cost of following Jesus as Lord and Savior. And again, fifty-four Fulani stood to receive Christ.

Clarice thought: *Perhaps the interpreter is misquoting me. The Fulani are resistant to the gospel!* So a third time, she presented the Good News. And new life sprang forth as again fifty-four stood to commit their lives to Jesus Christ.

How could such a tragedy turn into such a breakthrough for the Kingdom? Three months later the team found out. In Kona, Hawaii, a teacher (Asher Motola) at a Christian school gave his students an assignment to research an unreached people. One team of 11- to 14-year-olds chose the Fulani.

Gripped by the fact that very few missionaries were ministering to the Fulani, amazed at the fact that virtually no one was praying for the Fulani, the team of students made up a flyer urging prayer for this people group. They recruited 35 adults who committed themselves in writing to pray for the Fulani during a specific period of time. And that time, of course, was when Baby Rebecca died, and when 54 Fulani came to faith in Jesus Christ!

Opening Prayer

Lead in prayer for these new Fulani believers. Thank the Lord that He has since blessed the Brazilian couple with a new baby. And thank Him that your class, like the children in Kona, can be part of God's global plan.

ALTERNATE FOCUS BIBLE LEARNING ACTIVITY: A NEW WORLD MAP (6-8 MINUTES)

Direct your students to move their chairs or desks to the edge of the room. (This will get them up and moving in active involvement instead of stuck in the inertia that often settles in when they settle into their chairs.) Clear a space on the floor, or tape the sheets of butcher paper to a wall, or erase the chalkboard or white board. Put a dot at the left side of the upcoming map and announce:

This is *A Sunday for the World*, so we want to get an idea of what the world looks like. Each of you take a marker (crayon, or piece of chalk) and together begin drawing a gigantic world map. We want continents and countries labeled, plus any large cities you want to add. This dot represents our location. If you can't quite remember how something looks or the name of a country, just fake it and keep drawing. You've got four minutes to put the world together. Go!

Announce stop after four minutes. Direct students to rearrange their chairs as you critique their new world map. It's bound to be a pretty rough map, so have fun with this as the hubbub of activity settles down.

Opening Prayer

If you have students accustomed to praying aloud, ask a few to pray for the people in the places they drew on the map. Follow up these student prayers—or simply lead in prayer—by asking the Lord to give your class a clear picture of His heart for every people across the world today.

DISCOVER (15-18 MINUTES)

The learning activities in this section are designed to help your students discover what God says in the Bible.

Bible Study Word Games: People-Group Thinking (5-8 Minutes)

Pass out Student Worksheets and direct students to work in pairs on the Bible Study Word Games. One looks up a reference while the other fills in the answers. Then they trade roles. Move around the classroom to help children who are new to the Bible locate the verses.

Answers:

The Theme for *A Sunday for the World*

1. Look up Genesis 12:1-3. Fill in the blanks: God said, "I will _____bless_____ you... and you will be a _____blessing_____ to all the _____peoples_____."

2. Trace a line through the correct order of letters from the "I" to the "Genesis 12:1-3" reference.

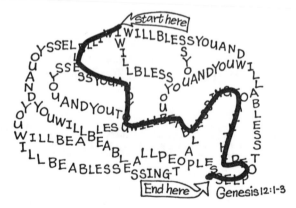

Why Does God Bless Us?

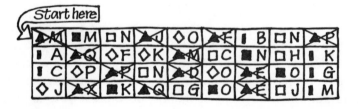

<u>M</u> <u>N</u> <u>O</u> <u>B</u> <u>N</u> <u>A</u> <u>F</u> <u>K</u> <u>C</u> <u>N</u> <u>H</u> <u>K</u> <u>C</u> <u>P</u> <u>N</u> <u>O</u> <u>O</u> <u>G</u> <u>I</u> <u>K</u> <u>G</u> <u>O</u> <u>I</u> <u>M</u>

Why does God bless us?

So that we will be <u>salvation</u> <u>among</u> <u>the</u> <u>peoples</u>.

Who Are We Talking About?

1. Look up Matthew 28:19. Who are we commanded to make disciples of and teach? All _____nations_____

2. The New Testament was originally written in the Greek language. In Greek, the word in the blank in question 1 is ethne. The maze below tells us clearly who we're supposed to bless, disciple and teach. Follow each letter through the maze to find the answer. All the_____ethnic_____ _____groups_____

From the Tower of Babel to Today

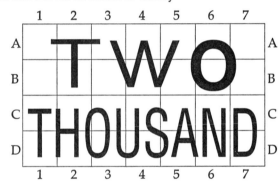

2. These are the people groups who now don't know about Jesus. Look up Revelation 5:9. How many of them will some day have at least one person in heaven? _____All_____

3. If you have time, look up Genesis 10 and count how many peoples or nations were formed at the Tower of Babel. _____70_____

   After 7-8 minutes, read very quickly the answers to the word puzzles and announce the Sword Drill.

Demonstration: You, a Priest (10 Minutes)

Be sure each student has a Bible. Announce an old fashioned Sword Drill:

Say **Since the Bible is the Sword of the Spirit, we'll practice using it in a Sword Drill. Hold your Bibles up. When I announce a reference, look it up. The first person to find it is to jump up and read the verse. If you'd rather have me read it, I will once I'm sure you've actually found the right verse. Ready?**

- Exodus 19:5,6;
- 1 Peter 2:9.

Say These two passages are talking about the same thing—that God's people are a nation of priests, that we have a royal priesthood. Turn to a neighbor and greet him or her with the title of priest.

Demonstrate quickly and simply by greeting students: **Hello, priest Jason. Hello, priest Megan.** Etc.

Ask **What does a priest do?**

If your students are unfamiliar with the historic Tabernacle or Temple, draw on the board a simple diagram of the layout. (Refer to the following sketch of the actual layout.)

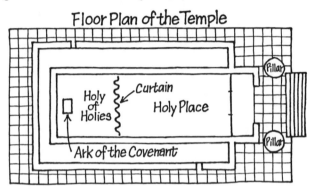

Act out as you ad lib the following:

We get a good picture from the Old Testament of what a priest does. Once a year, the high priest would get pretty nervous, walk to the Tabernacle or Temple and go into the holy place. There an assistant would help him into an ornate robe with little bells around the bottom. The first bell-bottoms, right? Another would help tie a big rope around the priest's ankle. Then he would clear his throat...and stepping through the veil he would enter the holy of holies!

As he would do his priestly stuff, the attendants outside would listen carefully to the jingling of the bells as he moved. And they'd panic if the jingling stopped. Why were they all so nervous about the priest entering into the holy of holies? Because if there were unconfessed sin in his life, he would be—wham!—struck dead! And nobody would want to go in after him, so they would drag him out by pulling on the rope. Not very dignified for a high priest!

But what would the priest do in the holy of holies? He would sprinkle the blood of the sacrifices on the mercy seat, as a picture of the coming Messiah whose blood would be shed to cleanse us from sin. And he would pray for a higher salary, right? For new sandals, for his sore toe. No. He would pray for the people. That's the first job of a priest: Pray for others.

Then, after he would come out of the holy of holies, he would serve the people. He would take the sacrificed meat and pass it out so the people could enjoy a feast.

Those are the two things a priest does: Prays for others and serves others. And since we as the people of God are a whole nation of priests, our job is first to pray for the peoples of the world and second, to serve them in the name of Jesus.

Before we leave today we'll act out our role as priests and pray for some of the world's people groups who don't know Jesus Christ.

And let's pray that each of you will find out how to serve—whether it's here blessing the people of our own country or blessing another people group somewhere across the world.

ALTERNATE DISCOVER BIBLE LEARNING ACTIVITY

Blessed to Bless the Peoples: A Synchronized Reading and Taping (15-18 Minutes)

Designed for Grade 6 or other students who are mature readers, this activity gets your class into the Word. It also prepares a reading which, via a recorded cassette, lets your pastor in on what your class has learned today.

If you choose this activity, your class won't need the Student Worksheet, just their copies of the "Synchronized Reading Script" parts below. Don't try to explain all of the steps of this activity to your class all at once; simply direct them step-by-step.

- Assign parts: Each student is to be assigned one of the four parts as noted on the "Synchronized Reading Script." If you have fewer than four in your class, read one or more of the parts yourself. If you have more than four, assign several students to the same part.

- Fill in the blanks: Allow just three to five minutes for students to look up their two or three verses and fill in the six blanks designated for their parts in the script. Move about the room to be available if a student can't find a reference or determine what to put in a blank.

Below is the finished script (using *NASB*, *NIV* and *KJV* translations). Varying translations will produce slightly different wordings for a student's answers. (This will not affect the reading presentation.) Basically the finished script is:

Synchronized Reading Script

"Blessed to Bless the Peoples"

In the beginning, God told Adam and Eve and later the family of Noah: "Be fruitful and multiply, and fill the earth" (Genesis 1:28; 9:1,7). Instead they began to build a city with a great tower to rebel against God. They said, "Let us make a name for ourselves and not be scattered over the face of the whole earth" (Genesis 11:4). So God confused their languages (see Genesis 11:7) at this tower of Babel and made them into separate nations. God made every nation of mankind and He "determined the times set for them, and the exact places where they should live" (Acts 17:26).

Out of these nations, God chose Abraham and said, first, "I will surely bless you," (Genesis 22:17) and, second, "Through your offspring all the nations of the earth will be blessed" (Genesis 22:18).

God blesses us to bless the nations. The Bible says, "God be gracious to us and bless us, and make His face to shine upon us—that Thy way may be known among the nations, Thy salvation among all peoples" (Psalm 67:1,2). (In the Bible, the nations are sometimes called peoples or the Gentiles.) "God blesses us, that all the ends of the earth may fear Him" (Psalm 67:7).

God promises that His "name will be great among the nations" (Malachi 1:11). He keeps a big book, a register of the peoples (see Psalm 87:6) to make sure each people group is blessed with His offer of salvation. Will all of these nations or peoples say yes to Christ? Some men, women, boys and girls in each people group will become believers in Jesus Christ, because around Jesus' throne in heaven there will be some from every tribe and language and people and nation (see Revelation 5:9). In the people groups where more and more become Christians, they will know that "Blessed is the nation whose God is the Lord" (Psalm 33:12).

How can we bless the peoples of the world? One way is to be priests for them. In the Old Testament, God's people were to be a whole kingdom of priests to pray for and serve among all the world's peoples (see Exodus 19:5,6). New Testament Christians today are a royal priesthood that we may proclaim the excellencies of Him (see 1 Peter 2:9) who has called us out of darkness into His marvelous light (see 1 Peter 2:9).

As a Christian, I am a royal priest. My job is to pray for and serve the peoples of the world. Right now I can pray. And I can serve, too, because even in my own country there are many different people groups. Besides, one of the people groups that needs to be blessed is my own. In my future, I can keep praying, and maybe I'll go to another people in another part of the world to "*let the peoples praise Thee,...let all the peoples praise Thee, let the nations be glad and sing for joy*" (Psalm 67:3,4, italics added).

- Practice the synchronized reading. Point out the instructions on each script. Each student is to read only the words in bold print plus the words he or she filled in the blanks. Move slowly through your first readings, allowing for the natural awkwardness of choral reading. Read through several more times—perhaps three or four times—until all feel comfortable with the presentation.
- Turn on the tape recorder and record the reading. Greet your pastor and introduce your readers. Give the reading's title "Blessed to Bless the Peoples," and then let your students do their best. (Don't expect perfection. This activity is more for your students' benefit than your pastor's. Even if disrupted by laughter or groans, finish the reading without resorting to several tapings—which would only waste your class time.) Assign a few of the students to deliver the cassette personally to your pastor later in the day.

DECIDE (10-12 MINUTES)

This Bible Learning Activity helps students apply the Bible lesson.

The Tower of Babel Prayer Reminder

Set out large sheets of paper (construction paper, legal-size paper or pieces of butcher paper), scissors, tape and marking pens or crayons.

Give the following directions several times in varying wording: **We saw that humans were divided into people groups at the Tower of Babel. What do you suppose that tower looked like? How tall was it? Did it have stairways, balconies, rooms inside it with big windows looking out, a big platform on the top? We don't really know.**

But with these sheets of paper we're going to make models of what we think the Tower of Babel looked like.

- You can make it any way you'd like as long as it can stand up on a flat surface.
- Color it, decorate it, anything—but leave three squares blank somewhere on it since we'll write something on them later.
- If you finish making your tower, pair up with a neighbor, turn to Genesis chapter 10 and start writing on your towers all the names of the people groups—the nations—that were formed at the Tower of Babel. See how many you can list. Be sure to leave three blank squares somewhere on your tower.

Allow about 8 to 10 minutes for students to finish their towers. Expect that some will throw together something in 60 seconds while others will still be carefully etching in window curtains by the end of the allowed time.

Say There were about 70 people groups formed at the Tower of Babel. Did any of you list them all? Today there are about 24,000 people groups. And some of these really need our prayers. Since we're priests, let's remind each other to pray this week for at least three of the unreached people groups of the world. Stick your tower somewhere where you'll see it. It will remind you that humankind is basically rebellious to God. But God still loves every people. Here are three people groups to put into the three squares you left blank on your towers. Remember this week to pray for...

Write on the chalkboard, overhead or flipchart the following people groups:

Throughout West Africa—The Fulani people
In Turkmenistan—The Turkmen people
In Mali, West Africa—The Bozos people

Point out West Africa and Turkmenistan (a former Soviet republic at the southeast corner of the Caspian Sea) on a world map or a rough sketch of a world map. Have fun mentioning the third sample people group; your students just might remember to pray for them for years to come.

Optional Input:

- Feel free to substitute any unreached people group for one or more of the above. Perhaps list an unreached group your fellowship is already focusing on in prayer.
- Listing "In the U.S.—The Anglo-American people group" or "The African-American people group" might be a good teaching point to help your students realize we're to intercede and serve even reached peoples.
- Listing "In Canada—The Hakka Chinese people" or "In Iraq and London, England—The Kurdish people" might help reinforce biblical people-group-thinking of God's global enterprise rather than the traditional geographical-country-based thinking.
- This might be a time to mention that although it is extremely

important for us to pray for missionaries working among another people group, it is also extremely important to pray for the people group itself—even when the missionaries come home.

ALTERNATE DECIDE ACTIVITIES (10-12 MINUTES)

This alternate Bible Learning Activity follows the Discover Alternate Bible Learning Activity. It helps your students consider applications of the Synchronized Reading Bible passages.

Compiling Answers (8-10 Minutes)

Have each student read the answers for the blanks of his part of the Synchronized Reading so the other students can fill in the appropriate blanks. For example, a student with the script for part one will read answers for blanks one through six. The other students will fill in these blanks as the answers are given. Don't be surprised if, because of your Synchronized Reading repetitions, most of the students are able to fill in all the blanks from memory.

Explain or amplify answers as you see fit from your personal study and reading of the Lesson Commentary.

A Mini-Registry of the Peoples (2 Minutes)

Wrap up this segment by listing on the chalkboard, overhead or flipchart the following people groups. Point out West Africa and Turkmenistan (a former Soviet republic at the southeast corner of the Caspian Sea) on a world map or a rough sketch of a world map. Have fun mentioning the third sample people group; your students just might remember to pray for them for years to come.

Say **God loves every people. Here are three people groups to pray for this week:**

Throughout West Africa—The Fulani people;

In Turkmenistan—The Turkmen people;

In Mali, West Africa—The Bozos people.

Optional Input:

- Feel free to substitute any unreached people group for one or more of the above. Perhaps list an unreached group your fellowship is already focusing on in prayer.
- Listing "In the U.S.—The Anglo-American people group" or "The African-American people group" might be a good teaching point to help your students realize we're to intercede and serve even reached peoples.
- Listing "In Canada—The Hakka Chinese people" or "In Iraq and London, England—The Kurdish people" might help reinforce biblical people-group-thinking of God's global enterprise rather than the traditional geographical-country-based thinking.
- This might be a time to mention that although it is extremely important for us to pray for missionaries working among another people group, it is also extremely important to pray for the people group itself—even when the missionaries come home.

DO (2-3 MINUTES)

This segment of your lesson is designed to help students act on what they've learned.

Written Prayers for the Peoples

Say We as God's people are a nation of priests, right? We're to pray for and serve all the people groups of the world. But before we can do that, we need to be sure there is no unconfessed sin in our lives. Let's bow for just a half minute and ask God to forgive us and cleanse us of anything that God brings to our minds.

Allow only about half a minute for silent prayer. Longer silences aren't handled well by most children.

Say If you know Jesus as your Savior, you are one of the people of God; you're part of a royal priesthood. Since you're a priest, it's time to pray for the people groups of the world. Pick one of the people groups we listed and write a sentence prayer for them on a piece of paper. Then hand it in to me. After a minute I'll read these prayers. You don't need to put your name on the paper.

Allow time for your class to jot down their prayers. Expect that some may simply write the name of a people—which is all right. Then say:

In many parts of the world, believers don't close their eyes and bow their heads to pray. Often they keep their eyes open and look upward. You do that now, and pray silently along with me as I read these prayers.

In your prayer, praise the Lord that He has let us be priests for the whole world. Then simply pray the students' prayers and close with your own prayer.

Make sure each student has a Family Activity Guide.

ALTERNATE DO BIBLE LEARNING ACTIVITY (2-3 MINUTES)

Choose this Bible Learning Activity if you have more time. It will help reinforce the message of the lesson in your mind as well as your students' minds.

Blessed to Be a Blessing

Repeat the "Psalm 67 Song" on the Family Activity Guide until your class learns it from memory. Be sure each student has a Family Activity Guide to take home after you close in prayer.

SYNCHRONIZED READING SCRIPT

BLESSED TO BLESS THE PEOPLES

Reading Part 1

1. Look up the passages to fill in blanks 1-6.
2. When your whole class starts reading the script, **read only the words in bold print and the words you put in blanks 1-6.** Do not read the Scripture references.

In the beginning, God told Adam and Eve and later the family of Noah: "Be fruitful and multiply and (1) _____" (Genesis 1:28; 9:1,7). **Instead they began to build a city with a great tower to rebel against God. They said,** "Let us make (2)_____ and not be (3)_____" (Genesis 11:4). So God (4)_____ their _____(see Genesis 11:7) at this tower of **Babel** and made them into separate nations. **God made every nation of mankind and He** "determined (5)_____, and (6)_____" (Acts 17:26).

Out of these nations, God chose Abraham and said **first** "I will surely (7)_____," (Genesis 22:17) **and second,** (8) "_____ all the (9)_____ **will be blessed**" (Genesis 22:18).

God blesses us to bless the nations. The Bible says, "**God be gracious to us and** (10)_____ and make His face to shine upon us **that** (11)_____, **Thy salvation among** (12)_____" (Psalm 67:1,2). **(In the Bible, the nations are** sometimes called *peoples* or the *Gentiles.)* (13) "_____ that all the ends of the earth may fear Him" (Psalm 67:7).

God promises that His "name will be great (14)_____" (Malachi 1:11). He keeps a big book, a register of the (15)_____ (see Psalm 87:6) **to make sure each people group is blessed with His offer of salvation.** Will all of these nations **or peoples say yes to Christ?** Some men, women, **boys** and girls in each people group **will become believers in Jesus Christ,** because **around Jesus' throne in heaven there will be some from every** (16) "_____" (Revelation 5:9). **In the people groups where more and more become** Christians, they will know that "**Blessed is the** (17)_____ whose (18)_____" (Psalm 33:12).

How can we bless the **peoples of the world?** One way is to be **priests for them.** In the Old Testament, **God's people were to be a whole** (19)_____ (see Exodus 19:5,6) to pray for and serve among **all the world's peoples. New Testament Christians today** are a royal (20)_____ that we may (21)_____ (see 1 Peter 2:9) who has called us **out of darkness into His marvelous light.**

As a Christian, I am a royal priest. My job is **to pray for and serve the peoples of the world. Right now** I can pray. And I can serve now, too, **because even in my own country** there are many different **people groups. Besides, one of the people groups that needs to be blessed is my own.** In my future, I can keep **praying, and maybe I will go** to another people in another part of the world to "let (22)_____, let (23)_____ the peoples praise Thee, let (24)_____ be glad **and sing for joy**" (Psalm 67:3,4).

SYNCHRONIZED READING SCRIPT

Grades 4-6

BLESSED TO BLESS THE PEOPLES

Reading Part 2

1. Look up the passages to fill in <u>blanks 7-12</u>.
2. When your whole class starts reading the script, **read only the words in bold print and the words you put in blanks 7-12**. Do not read the Scripture references.

In the beginning, **God told** Adam **and** Eve **and later the family of** Noah: **"Be fruitful and multiply and** (1)_____" (Genesis 1:28; 9:1,7). Instead they began to build a city **with a great tower to rebel against God.** They said, **"Let us make** (2)_____ **and not be** (3)_____**"** (Genesis 11:4). So God (4)_____ **their** _____ (see Genesis 11:7) **at this tower of Babel and made them into** separate nations. **God** made every nation of mankind **and He** "determined (5)_____, **and** (6)_____" (Acts 17:26).

Out of these nations, God chose Abraham and said first **"I will surely** (7)_____," (Genesis 22:17) and **second,** (8)"_____ **all the** (9)_____ **will be blessed"** (Genesis 22:18).

God **blesses us** to **bless** the nations. The Bible says, "God be gracious to us **and** (10)_____ and make His face to shine upon us **that** (11)_____, Thy **salvation among** (12)_____**"** (Psalm 67:1,2). (In the Bible, **the nations are sometimes called** *peoples* **or the** *Gentiles.*) (13) "_____ **that** all the ends of the earth may **fear** Him" (Psalm 67:7).

God promises **that His** "name **will be great** (14)_____" (Malachi 1:11). He keeps a big book, a register of the (15)_____ (see Psalm 87:6) to make sure **each people group** is blessed with His offer of salvation. Will all of these nations or peoples say yes to Christ? Some men, **women,** boys and girls in each people group will become believers in Jesus Christ, **because around Jesus' throne in heaven there will be some from every** (16) "_____" (Revelation 5:9). In the people groups where **more and more become Christians,** they will know that "Blessed is the (17)_____ **whose** (18)_____" (Psalm 33:12).

How can we bless the peoples of the world? One way is to be priests for them. **In the Old Testament,** God's people were to be a whole (19)_____ (see Exodus 19:5,6) **to pray for and serve among all the world's peoples.** New Testament Christians today are a royal (20)_____ **that we may** (21)_____ (1 Peter 2:9) **who has called us out of darkness into His marvelous light.** As a Christian, **I am a royal priest.** My job is to pray for and serve the peoples of the world. Right now I can pray. **And I can serve now, too,** because even in my own country there **are many different people groups. Besides, one of the people groups that needs to be blessed is my own. In my future, I can keep** praying, and **maybe I will go** to another people in another **part of the world** to "let (22)_____, **let** (23)_____ the peoples praise Thee, let (24)_____ be glad and **sing for joy"** (Psalm 67:3,4).

SYNCHRONIZED READING SCRIPT

BLESSED TO BLESS THE PEOPLES

Reading Part 3

1. Look up the passages to fill in <u>blanks 13-18</u>.
2. When your whole class starts reading the script, **read only the words in bold print and the words you put in blanks 13-18.** Do not read the Scripture references.

In the beginning, **God told Adam** and Eve and later the **family of Noah: "Be fruitful and multiply and** (1)_____" (Genesis 1:28; 9:1,7). Instead they began to build a city with a great tower **to rebel against God. They said, "Let us make** (2)_____**and not be** (3)_____**"** (Genesis 11:4). So God (4)_____their _____(see Genesis 11:7) at this tower of **Babel** and made them into **separate nations. God** made every nation **of mankind and He "determined** (5)_____, and (6)_____" (Acts 17:26).

Out of these nations, **God** chose Abraham **and said** first **"I will surely** (7)_____**,"** (Genesis 22:17) and second, (8)**"**_____**all the** (9)_____**will be blessed"** (Genesis 22:18).

God blesses us to **bless** the nations. The Bible says, **"God be gracious to us and** (10)_____**and make His face to shine upon us that** (11)_____, Thy salvation among (12)_____**"** (Psalm 67:1,2). (In the Bible, the nations are sometimes called *peoples* or the *Gentiles*.) (13) "_____that all the ends of the earth **may fear Him"** (Psalm 67:7).

God promises that His **"name will be great** (14)_____**"** (Malachi 1:11). He keeps a big book, **a register of the** (15)_____(see Psalm 87:6) to make sure each people group is blessed with **His offer of salvation.** Will all of these nations or peoples say yes to Christ? **Some men,** women, boys and girls **in each people group will become believers** in Jesus Christ, because around Jesus' throne in heaven **there will be some from every** (16) "_____**"** (Revelation 5:9). In the people groups where more and **more become Christians,** they will know that **"Blessed is the** (17)_____ **whose** (18)_____**"** (Psalm 33:12).

How can we bless the peoples of the world? One way is to be priests for them. In the Old Testament, **God's people were to be a whole** (19)_____ (see Exodus 19:5,6) to pray for **and serve among all the world's peoples.** New Testament Christians today **are a royal** (20)_____ that we may (21)_____ (see 1 Peter 2:9) **who has called us out of darkness into His marvelous light.**

As a Christian, I am a royal priest. **My job is** to pray for **and serve** the peoples of the world. Right now I can pray. And I can serve now, too, because even in my own country there **are many different people groups.** Besides, one of the people groups **that needs to be blessed is my own.** In my future, **I can keep** praying, **and maybe I will go to another people in another part of the world to** "let (22)_____, let (23)_____ **the peoples praise Thee, let** (24)_____ **be glad and sing for joy"** (Psalm 67:3,4).

SYNCHRONIZED READING SCRIPT

Grades 4-6

BLESSED TO BLESS THE PEOPLES

Reading Part 4

1. Look up the passages to fill in blanks 19-24.
2. When your whole class starts reading the script, **read only the words in bold print and the words you put in blanks 19-24.** Do not read the Scripture references.

In the beginning, **God** told Adam and **Eve** and later the family of Noah: "**Be fruitful and multiply** and (1)_____" (Genesis 1:28; 9:1,7). Instead they began to build a city with a great tower to rebel against God. They said, "**Let us make** (2)_____**and not be** (3)_____" (Genesis 11:4). So God (4)_____their _____(see Genesis 11:7) at this tower of **Babel** and made them into separate nations. **God made every nation of mankind** and He "determined (5)_____, and (6)_____" (Acts 17:26).

Out of these nations, **God chose Abraham and said** first "**I will surely** (7)_____," (Genesis 22:17) and second, (8) "_____ all the (9)_____**will be blessed**" (Genesis 22:18).

God **blesses us** to bless **the nations. The Bible says,** "God be gracious to us and (10)_____ and **make His face to shine upon us** that (11)_____, Thy salvation among (12)_____" (Psalm 67:1,2). (In the Bible, the nations are sometimes called *peoples* or the *Gentiles*.) (13) "_____that **all the ends of the earth** may fear Him" (Psalm 67:7).

God promises that **His "name will be great** (14)_____" (Malachi 1:11). He keeps a big book, a register of the (15)_____(see Psalm 87:6) to make sure each people group is blessed with His offer of salvation. **Will all of these nations** or peoples **say yes to Christ?** Some men, women, boys **and girls in each people group will become believers** in Jesus Christ, because around Jesus' throne in heaven there will be some from every (16) "_____" (Revelation 5:9). In the people groups where more and more become Christians, **they will know that "Blessed is the** (17)_____ whose (18)_____" (Psalm 33:12).

How can we **bless the peoples of the world?** One way is to be priests for them. In the Old Testament, God's people were to be a whole (19)_____ (see Exodus 19:5,6) to pray for and serve among **all the world's peoples.** New Testament Christians today **are a royal** (20)_____ that we may **proclaim** (21)_____ (see 1 Peter 2:9) who has called us out of darkness into His marvelous light. As a Christian, I am a royal **priest.** My job is to pray for and serve the peoples of the world. Right now **I can pray. And I can serve now, too,** because even in my own country **there are many different people groups.** Besides, one of the people groups that needs to be blessed is **my own.** In my future, I can keep praying, and maybe I will go **to another people in another part of the world** to "let (22)_____, let (23)_____ **the peoples praise Thee, let** (24)_____ be glad and **sing for joy**" (Psalm 67:3,4).

STUDENT WORKSHEET

THE THEME FOR *A SUNDAY FOR THE WORLD*

1. Look up Genesis 12:1-3. Fill in the blanks: God said, "I will _____ you and you will be a _____ to all the _____."

2. Trace a line through the correct order of letters from the "I" to the "Genesis 12:1-3" reference.

WHY DOES GOD BLESS US?

1. Cross out the letters that have a triangle in front of them. Write the remaining letters in the order they appear to find the coded word.

2. Use the Decoder chart below to discover exactly why God blesses us.

3. Check your answer in an important *A Sunday for the World* passage—Psalm 67:1,2.

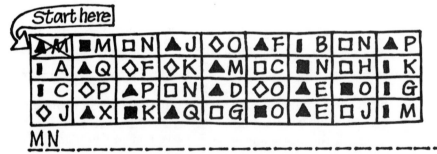

MN _____

Code Letter	A	H	K	F	M	J	G	B	O	P	N	C
↕ Actual Letter	T	M	O	I	S	E	P	V	L	G	A	N

So that there will be _ _ _ _ _ _ _ _ _ _ _ _ _ _ _ _.

WHO ARE WE TALKING ABOUT?

1. Look up Matthew 28:19. Who are we commanded to make disciples of and teach? All

   _____

2. The New Testament was originally written in the Greek language. In Greek, the word in the blank in question 1 is *ethne*. The maze below tells us clearly who we are supposed to bless, disciple and teach. Follow each letter through the maze to find the answer. All the _ _ _ _ _ _ _ _ _ _ _ _

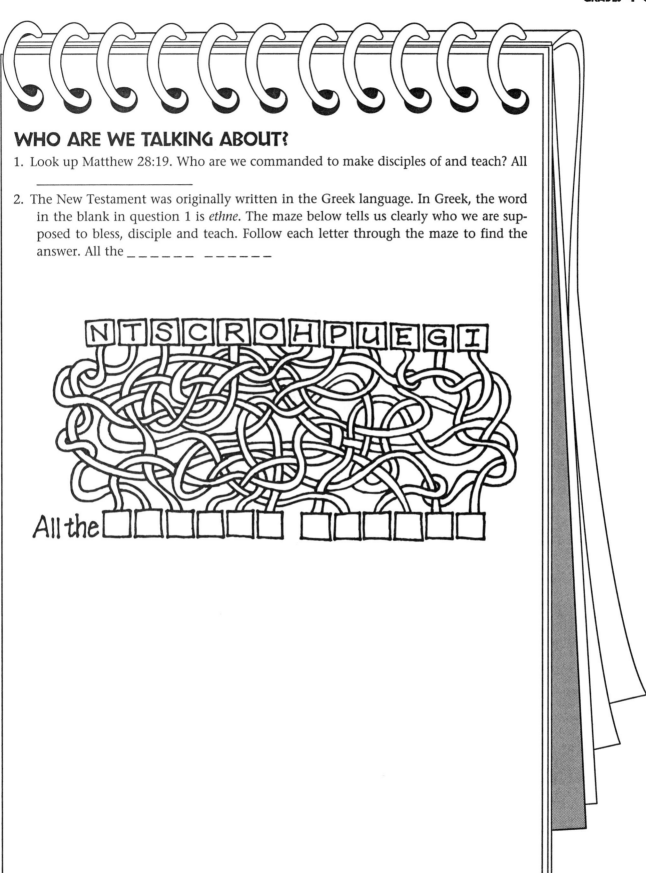

FROM THE TOWER OF BABEL TO TODAY

Genesis 10 lists the original number of people groups on the earth. Today how many people groups are there who have no idea God wants to bless them in Jesus Christ?

1. To find the answer, copy exactly the lines from the top squares into the correct boxes in the bottom squares.

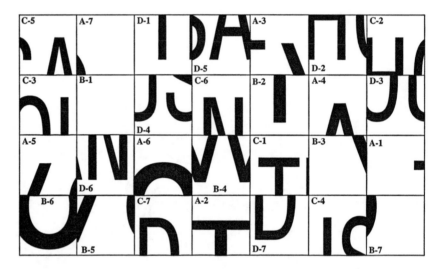

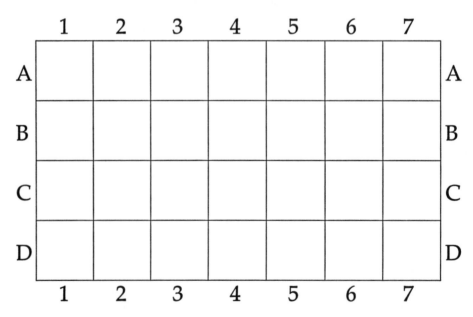

2. These are the people groups who now don't know about Jesus. Look up Revelation 5:9. How many of them will some day have at least one person in heaven?

_____

3. If you have time, look up Genesis 10 and count how many people or nations were formed at the Tower of Babel. _____

BOZOS AND ROCKETS

KEY VERSE

"You were slain, and with your blood you purchased men for God...from every tribe and language and people and nation." Revelation 5:9, *NIV*

KEY BIBLE PASSAGES

Genesis 12:1-3; 18:18; 22:17,18; 26:4; 28:14; 2 Chronicles 6:32,33; Psalm 67:1,2,7; Malachi 1:11; Matthew 28:19; Luke 2:29-32; 24:45-47; Romans 1:5; Revelation 5:9

OVERVIEW

God is moving worldwide today, but then, He's been doing it all along on a global scale: His blessing of every people is a theme we see throughout Scripture. As we understand more clearly what God is doing, we can find our part in His great plan. We'll find our specific role in one of the four basic dynamics of the overall mission of the church.

AIMS

In this session, we're not so much interested in conveying information as in generating an emotional response. Your teenagers will, as a result of this session:

- Know some of what God is doing worldwide, and how that fits with the biblical theme of God's blessing the nations;
- Feel surprise at what is happening outside their own worlds, and feel curious about where they fit;
- Act out a blessing on one of the world's people groups.

LESSON COMMENTARY

Don't even think about trying to share all this information with your students. This is background commentary for you as you prepare.

HMMMM?!?

Could God actually use His people to reach every person on earth with the good news of salvation? In the late 1800s, a British military official was asked how long it would take to get a message from Queen Victoria to every person on earth. He scratched his head, pondered the strategies, and replied in all seriousness, "Two years." Today the Coca-Cola Company has very realistic plans to put a Coke in the hand of every person on earth by the year 2000.

If God's people were a bit better clued in to what God has said in

His Word about strategy and into what He's doing in our world today, what might our answer be to the question: Can the claims of Christ actually be presented to the world?

The answer is yes. As the gospel penetrates an ethnic group within a country, new believers can be taught immediately to share the Good News with perhaps two of their relatives and neighbors. Some of those would respond with faith in Christ. And they in turn would be discipled to share with a couple more of their own people.

If that simple strategy were implemented, every person on earth would be personally presented the gospel within just a few years' time.

The key, of course, is penetrating every distinct grouping of people with the gospel and teaching them to duplicate themselves. But that's exactly the strategy God has outlined in Scripture. And, except in the West, it is being implemented in much of the rest of the world:

- The Body of Christ in China grew from about one million in 1949 to as many as 80 to 100 million today.
- Every day another 34,000 are added to the Body in Latin America.
- In Africa, churches are multiplying so rapidly that half the continent's population will claim Jesus Christ as Lord and Savior by the year 2000.
- David Wang of Asia Outreach International says of the revivals and spiritual movements in Asia: "We don't even call it a harvest anymore. We call it 'the great in-gathering.'"

See other encouraging breakthroughs on the following "Global Breakthroughs" sheet you'll cut apart and hand out to your students.

God is doing something awesome in our world today.

BACK TO THE BIBLE

But then He's always been doing awesome things. A quick sprint through Scripture reveals a theme not often noticed in Christianity that is sometimes only me-centered.

Sometimes we treat the Word as if it were a school yearbook. When you receive your yearbook, whose picture do you look for first? Your own, of course. And unfortunately, that's the way many of us look at the Book: If it's not about me, it's not very interesting. If it doesn't have a good promise or immediate personal application, I won't bother reading further. For example, most of us can quote what we think is the rest of "Be still, and..." from Psalm 46:10, *NIV*. But why do we never hear the actual rest of the verse?

Yes, the Book is about us. But we miss so much when we ignore the fact that it's primarily about Him—about what He is doing in history.

What is He doing? He's making strategic breakthroughs into every ethnic group on the earth. And He's deigned to use us ordinary believers, His people, to do it.

Let's glance at the biblical strategy:

- Genesis 12:1-3—God blessed Abraham and promised blessing to all families of the earth;
- Genesis 18:18—God blessed Abraham and promised blessing to all families or peoples of the earth;

102

- Genesis 22:17,18—God again blessed Abraham and promised blessing to all nations of the earth (see note in box);
- Genesis 26:4—God blessed Isaac and promised blessing to all peoples of the earth;
- Genesis 28:14—God blessed Jacob and promised blessing to all peoples of the earth.

By now it's obvious God wants us to notice this two-part program of blessing:

1. He will bless His people and
2. Through His people He will offer blessing to every unit of humanity on the planet.

Let's look at a few more passages:

- 2 Chronicles 6:32,33—The temple was for all peoples so "that all peoples of the earth may know [His] name";
- Psalm 67:1,2,7—The passage is startlingly clear: God blesses His people to be a blessing to every people group on the face of the earth:

"God be gracious to us and bless us,

And cause His face to shine upon us—

That Thy way may be known on the earth,

Thy salvation among all nations. . . .

God blesses us,

That all the ends of the earth may fear Him"

(Psalm 67:1,2,7)

- Malachi 1:11—God will accomplish His purpose of blessing every people;
- Matthew 28:19—The nations (*ethne* in the original Greek, from which we get our English word *ethnic*) are our focus;
- Luke 2:29-32—Jesus was born as a Light to bless all people groups (Gentiles) as well as to bless the Jews;
- Luke 24:45-47—Jesus emphasized Scripture's theme that the gospel is to be proclaimed to all nations or people groups;
- Romans 1:5—The nations are our focus;
- Revelation 5:9—God will accomplish His purpose of blessing every people. Some from every people will be present in eternity.

The basic point is: Throughout the Bible, God's plan is to bless His people and, through them, bless every people on the earth with the offer of redemption in Christ. Their responsibility, then, is to take that Good News to every individual in their society.

Where Do We Fit?

Think through the following illustration. God blesses us within the church—and He uses some of His people to do it.

Through the church, God offers blessing to our own people, our own society as some of us focus outside the church in our personal ministries.

And God uses some of us to bless other people groups. Some of these have church movements (Mexican, Russian, Korean, etc.). And

Note: The biblical term "nation" (as used today of the Cherokee nation) is not the same as a country. In the Bible, nations, peoples and families are often used interchangeably.

For example, within the political boundaries of the country of Mali are several distinct nations or ethnic groups which are separated by strong barriers of language, culture or acceptance.

One of those people groups in the West African country of Mali is—believe it or not—the Bozos. There will, of course, be bozos in heaven. (Fortunately, we'll love everybody then.) But these 70,000 real Bozo people will be represented in heaven—even though there is now absolutely no church among them. God promises that some from every people (see Revelation 5:9) will be there—including the Bozos. Pray for them now.

Note: This overview, naturally, raises many questions—which is why we're hosting *A Sunday for the World*.

The purpose of this Sunday's program is to raise curiosity about what God is doing today in the big picture and what our part is in it. With such a huge scope, we are obviously not going to answer every question. (To find out more on these topics, see For Further Study below as well as the Follow-up Action Steps and Resources in the *Sunday for the World* packet.)

some still don't (the Bozos [see box on page 103], Kurds, Bosnians, Somalis, Arabs of Saudi Arabia, etc.)

Where Do You Fit?

For Further Study:

- Read through *Catch the Vision 2000* by Bill and Amy Stearns (Bethany House, 1001). Available at Christian bookstores or call 800-MISSION.
- On your own or with a few friends, work through START, a study of God's global plan and your part in it. Available from Caleb Project, 10 W. Dry Creek Circle, Littleton, CO 80120-4170; Phone: 303-730-4170 Fax: 303-730-4177, Internet e-mail: Info@cproject.com.

LESSON PLAN

PREPARATION

1. Study the Bible passages listed and the material in your Lesson Commentary.
2. Pray that God will help your junior high students catch a vision of their places in God's global plan.
3. Think through the following Lesson Plan activities.
4. Prepare materials as listed.

MATERIALS NEEDED

- A Bible for each student;
- Pencils and color markers or crayons;
- A photocopy of the Student Worksheets for each expected student and visitor;
- Photocopy "Global Breakthroughs" and cut apart;
- If making rockets in the Decide activity, sheets of paper—from 8½ x 11 to 11 x 17, any colors, scissors, tape;
- A world map—particularly in the Focus activity (optional).

SESSION AT A GLANCE

Focus (10-12 Minutes)

A Sunday for the World News

Discover (12 Minutes)

Bible Blitz

Decide (20 Minutes)

Rockets

Oral Pop Quiz: Where You Wanna Fit?

Do (1-2 Minutes)

Prayer for the Nations

THE SESSION

AS STUDENTS ARRIVE

Greet students by handing each a Student Worksheet 1 and pencil. Encourage them to do the As You Arrive activity. (Read through the activity yourself first.)

FOCUS (10-12 MINUTES)

This opening activity is designed to hook your students' interest in God's global perspective.

A Sunday for the World News

1. Cut up "Global Breakthroughs" and give one to each student. (If you have more students than breakthroughs—bless your heart—have them work in pairs.)

   (Note: Read through these breakthroughs now and be prepared to explain any unfamiliar terms and point out geographical locations.)

2. Allow just three to four minutes for each student to prepare her or his news report. Then call for each to give a breakthrough.

   (Note: Be sensitive to students' reluctance to read aloud. Perhaps offer to be the announcer for a shy student's report. Many or most of the news reports will read suspiciously like the printed "Global Breakthrough" you have handed out. This plagiarism is okay; the point in this Focus activity is neither to prove their creativity nor to remember all the breakthrough statistics. It's to be generally impressed—even shocked—that God is doing so much that we in our quiet corner of Christianity don't know much about.)

Prayer

Thank God for what He is doing worldwide today. Pray that we'll each find our part in His plan.

DISCOVER (12 MINUTES)

The Discover activity is the heart of your session because it involves each learner directly in God's Word.

Bible Blitz

(Remember the old Bible Drill, sometimes called a Sword Drill? Just emphasize the word "Blitz" and your Junior Highers will never recognize it as something their grandparents did in Sunday School.)

Distribute Student Worksheet 2.

Transition to the Blitz by saying: **God is breaking through worldwide, and you get to grow up in these exciting days. But God has been breaking through to people all through history. Let's run through a Bible Blitz to get the idea: God promises to offer His blessing to every people group on earth.**

State the Blitz rules:

1. **I'll announce a Bible verse.** (If your students are shaky on Bible references and if you all have the same edition of Bibles, you might also announce the page number.)

2. **The first person to find the verse leap to your feet. I'll be the judge on any ties. Then read the verse or point it out on the page and I'll read it.**

3. **Then everyone write the reference on your Student Worksheet. Ready?**

- Genesis 12:1-3—God blessed Abraham and promised blessing to all families of the earth;
- Genesis 18:18—God blessed Abraham and promised blessing to all families or peoples of the earth;
- Genesis 22:17,18—God again blessed Abraham and promised blessing to all nations of the earth;
- Genesis 26:4—God blessed Isaac and promised blessing to all peoples of the earth;
- Genesis 28:14—God blessed Jacob and promised blessing to all peoples of the earth;
- Psalm 67:1,2,7—God blesses His people to be a blessing to every people group;
- Matthew 28:19—Disciple all the nations (*ethne*);
- Revelation 5:9—God will accomplish His purpose of blessing every people. Some from every people will be present in eternity.

Blitz through these references, adding brief comments gleaned from your own study and the Lesson Commentary. Be sure to emphasize over and over that God blesses His people to bless every people—every culture.

To wrap up this activity, say **God wants everybody to know they can be blessed to go to heaven. Is it really possible to let everybody in every people group know about Jesus Christ? Did any of you figure out a good plan in the As You Arrive question?** Allow responses, then simply suggest that: **Today we can get an important announcement to every country. Then each country can make sure that within its borders every people group (tribe, clan, language group) gets the announcement. Then each people group is responsible for getting that announcement to each family and individual. Jesus' Great Commission is do-able.**

DECIDE (20 MINUTES)

This activity helps your learners begin to think about their parts in God's plan for all peoples.

Rockets

Help your students make their own four-stage rockets:

1. Twist a sheet of paper into a narrow cone and tape in place.
2. Cut squarely across the bottom of the cone so it will stand on a tabletop.
3. Cut three triangles and tape as fins at the base of the rocket.

4. Draw lines to give the rocket four stages.

5. Decorate each stage with colored markers.

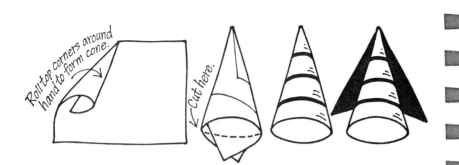

Roll top corners around hand to form cone.

Cut here.

Alternate: If you don't want to have your class produce rockets, simply draw a large four-stage rocket on the chalkboard or flipchart. Ask one student at a time to come to the board and, while you're talking about a particular stage, decorate that stage with any kind of markings he or she desires. Use information from your own study and from the Lesson Commentary to briefly talk about each stage—each dynamic—of the rocket—the overall mission of the Church.

Oral Pop Quiz: Where You Wanna Fit?

If you used the Alternate activity above, move right into the Pop Quiz, asking specific students for responses. (See note in box.)

If your students made rockets, while they're still creating, draw the rocket chart (see Lesson Commentary) on the chalkboard, overhead or flipchart. (Step 5 above allows slower rocket scientists to finish the basic rocket while the quicker ones can decorate to their hearts' content.) When all have rockets, talk through the chart using ideas from the Lesson Commentary. Then ask various students the Pop Quiz questions.

Say **Your rocket's four stages are like the four ways God is blessing His people—true Christians—to bless every people. While we go through these stages of the rocket, I'll be giving you a dreaded Pop Quiz! Let's see how you do.**

Stage One: He uses some believers to bless His people—other believers within the church. Direct students to label the first stage **Bless the church.**

Pop quiz Question 1: What is one way Christians in the church bless other Christians? (Teaching, helping in the nursery, music groups, etc.)

Stage Two: God uses some believers to bless our own people group. Name your own people group, or, if you're multi-cultural as a group, name the groups represented such as Anglo-American, African-American, Cherokee, Khmer, Han Chinese, etc. Direct students to label the second stage of their rockets: **Bless my people group.**

Pop quiz Question 2: What is one way Christians can bless our own people? (Telling the Good News, helping the homeless, etc.)

Stage Three: God uses some believers to bless other people groups that already have churches. Direct students to label the third stage: **Bless other peoples that have churches.**

Note: If your students are reluctant to answer your oral questions in activities such as the Pop Quiz, don't try to punish them for not answering with a sort of power play in which everyone sits in boring, awkward silence. They're not bad if they don't want to answer, and you're not a bad teacher if you have got the typical Junior High class that doesn't like to respond.

Students don't answer for all kinds of reasons: They're embarrassed to be wrong, embarrassed to be right, smarting from an argument with a parent, needing to go to the bathroom, lost in space and missing the question, etc. Usually the most common reason for not answering your oral questions is they've been conditioned by school classroom protocol, where at this point in their lives it just isn't cool to respond to a teacher as if he or she is actually human.

You can gradually train your students to interact in your lessons by getting to know them well. They will want to help you out during lessons, and they will unknowingly interact with you, responding without realizing they're actually answering questions in a class setting. Here are some ways to develop interactive students:

- Notice details about them— whether they're tired, what they're wearing, what their latest hobby/fanatic interest is, etc.;
- Engage them in conversation in and outside of class;
- Use humor;
- Refer to real examples from their lives;
- Genuinely praise them as they do participate.

By the time you know students well enough to write a full-page biography on each of them, you'll find you'll be enjoying the rewards of genuine student/teacher interaction.

Pop quiz Question 3: **Name one other culture where lots of people are Christians.** (Mexican, Russian, Korean, etc.)

Stage Four: God uses some believers to bless other people groups that don't have any churches. Direct students to label the fourth stage: **Bless unreached peoples.**

Pop quiz Question 4: **Can you name a people group that still doesn't have any or many Christians?** (Kurds, Bosnians, Somali, Arabs of Saudi Arabia, etc. Be sure to mention the unusual unreached people group of Mali in West Africa—the Bozos.)

Pop quiz Question 5: **If you had to choose which stage you'd like to serve in, which would it be?** (Ask each member of the class for her or his choice.)

DO (1-2 MINUTES)

This closing prayer activity helps your learners practice what is probably their most strategic part in God's plan for all peoples.

Prayer for the Nations

Say **What's one very important way we can bless every people right now?** Through prayer. **Let's do as the 12 million Christians in the Middle East do when they pray. They don't bow their heads; they look up to heaven with their eyes open as if they're looking at Jesus. Let's pray that way. You repeat aloud after me: Dear Lord— Bless us—to bless every people in the world—like the Mongolians— and the Kurds—and the Bozos....** (Add to the prayer as the Lord leads.)

108

STUDENT WORKSHEET 1

AS YOU ARRIVE

Let's say a global strategy meeting decides to launch a space station that will represent all the world's cultures. But what should the space station's name be? You, galactic space expert, are called in to solve the problem. You advise the committee to ask every human on earth for a vote on a name. You're applauded for your brilliance.

Now, how will you get everybody on the planet to vote? Figure out a step-by-step plan, listing the steps below.

A SUNDAY FOR THE WORLD NEWS

Your teacher will give you a global breakthrough—something God is doing. On the back of this sheet write a newspaper headline and a couple of sentences of a news article or prepare a 30-second radio-style news break.

Example:

A SUNDAY FOR THE WORLD NEWS

LARGEST MEETING OF HUMANS IN HISTORY

Seoul, Korea—Two million seven hundred thousand Korean Christians joined together recently in prayer on a Saturday afternoon in Seoul. Millions of Korean Christians get up at 5 A.M. every day to pray for their country and for the world.

Example:

A SUNDAY FOR THE WORLD RADIO NEWS BREAK

I'm live from Croatia. In this new country that used to be part of Yugoslavia, the government just announced that the Bible will be taught in all public schools. For *"A Sunday for the World* Radio News," this is Herkimer Housermountain.

STUDENT WORKSHEET 2

BIBLE BLITZ

God has always been making news as He offers His blessing to all the world's people groups. Write down the reference for each item below.

- Bless you, bless every family: _____
- Bless you, bless every people: _____
- Bless you, bless every people: _____
- Bless you, bless every people: _____
- God blesses us to bless all peoples: _____
- Disciple all the nations (ethnic people groups): _____
- The gospel to all nations or people groups: _____
- Every people group represented in heaven: _____

THE ROCKET POP QUIZ

There are four stages—like the stages of a rocket—in what God is doing through Christians. Of the stages, I'd like to:

Stage One: ___ Strengthen our local church.

Stage Two: ___ Bless my own people group.

Stage Three: ___ Bless churches in other people groups that have churches.

Stage Four: ___ Be a missionary to an unreached people group.

PRAYER FOR THE NATIONS

One thing I can do now to help bless every people is_____.

I can also take home a Family Activity Guide with more stuff to do about my part in God's global plan.

GLOBAL BREAKTHROUGHS

- True Christianity has grown by more than 300 million believers in the past ten years. About 10 million of these new Christians are from North America and Europe, and the rest—290 million—are from developing countries like Nigeria, Argentina, India and China.

- The biggest group of Christians in Spain is the Evangelical Gypsy Church with about 200,000 believers. The Gypsies have sent out missionaries to Madagascar and South America.

- There's a seminary in Indonesia where to graduate you have to do all the schoolwork plus start a whole church plus see at least 15 Muslims come to faith in Jesus Christ. In the past 6 years, these students have started more than 600 churches and seen 40,000 Muslims find new life in Christ.

- There's a great revival sweeping across the islands of the South Pacific. In Vinuatu (vin-oo-ah-too) tourists can't walk down a village street without someone coming up and asking, "Do you know Jesus Christ?"

- In the Philippine Islands, a group of Christians gathered outside a stadium near Manila to publicly dedicate the Philippines to Jesus Christ. How many showed up? A million.

- Just north of China, Mongolia didn't have any meeting of Christians at all in 1990. But within four years, the number of believers had grown so much they sent their first two missionaries to spread the gospel in India.

- In Peru in South America, an American couple was ambushed by Shining Path guerrillas who beat them and stole their Jeep. Later the guerrillas found in the Jeep a generator, a film projector and film reels. Thinking the movies were *Batman* or *Jurassic Park*, the soldiers that night showed the film—which turned out to be the *Jesus* film. They were bored, so they watched it anyway. In fact, the whole camp of guerrillas watched the life of Jesus seven times in a row. And many of the soldiers laid down their weapons and went home to follow Jesus. The American couple learned of this when the leader of the ambush squad asked their forgiveness since he, too, had come to faith in Christ.

- God is sending out Navajo and Apache Indian cowboys from the United States to be short-term missionaries in places like Mongolia and Central Asia.

- In a Middle Eastern country where the government is against Christianity, the national newspaper published an article warning people about Christians promoting Bible study by mail. The newspaper showed a photograph of the Bible study ad including the address. And thousands of people, able to make out the address in the picture, enrolled that next month to study the Bible by mail.

- In a single summer in Mombasa, Kenya in East Africa, 56,000 Muslims came to faith in Jesus Christ.

- In one baptismal service in the ocean on the coast of Angola in southern Africa, 10,000 were baptized in one day.

- Every day around the world, another 174,000 are added to the Body of Christ.

- One thousand Puerto Rican young people are being trained to go as missionaries to the Muslims.

- Every month another 15,000 in India are baptized as new believers in Jesus Christ.

- Recently in Wichita, Kansas, 3,000 young people found new life in Christ in one weekend.

- Prayer groups are getting big. More than 2.7 million gathered at one time in Yoido Plaza in Seoul, Korea—the largest face-to-face meeting of humans in history. About 45,000 gathered

for prayer at the national soccer stadium in Guatemala City, Guatemala. And 26,000 gathered in the Blue Jay Stadium in Toronto, Canada to pray. In Southern California, about 300 high schoolers gather once a month to pray for the world. In October 1995, more than 30 million Christians prayed around the world for 100 key cities.

- More than 15,000 public school teachers in the former Soviet Union are now teaching morals from the Bible and the life of Christ in their classes.

- Every 14 days another translation of the New Testament is begun in a new language. If we're still here, at least some portion of the Bible will be translated into every language on earth by the year 2020.

- There are as many as 80 to 100 million true believers in Jesus Christ in China.

- In a recent year, the best-selling book in Japan was the Bible.

- Almost all the Bible-believing churches in England vowed to work together to start 20,000 new churches in the country by the year 2000.

- In March 1995, Billy Graham's teaching was broadcast by satellite to over 165 countries. One billion people heard the gospel and one million Christian workers had three days of training broadcasts.

- Recently a church in Guatemala sent its first construction and evangelism team to repair the homes of the poor and present the gospel each evening after work. The Guatemalan team was sent to Minneapolis, Minnesota.

- A church started in 1983 in Buenos Aires, Argentina now has 215,000 members.

- Some of the most effective people spreading the gospel today are a Filipino couple working under a Singapore mission agency, supported by an Indonesian church working among Indians in Paraguay, South America.

- God uses all kinds of things in His global plan—like comic book writers and artists. In December 1995, a conference in Manila in the Philippines met to plan massive production of Christian comic books to distribute by the millions across Asia, Africa and Latin America.

How can you find out more about these kinds of global breakthroughs? Use your e-mail to send a message to hub@xc.org and put as the message *Subscribe Brigada* (with nothing in the subject area). *Brigada* is the Russian word for network, and Christians around the world are networking on the Net.

WORLD-CLASS SPECIAL FX

KEY VERSE

"You were slain and with your blood you purchased men for God from every tribe and language and people and nation." Revelation 5:9, *NIV*

KEY BIBLE PASSAGES

Genesis 12:1-3; 18:18; 22:17,18; 26:4; 28:14; Deuteronomy 6:4; 2 Chronicles 6:32,33; Psalm 46:10; 67:1,2,7; Malachi 1:11; Matthew 28:19; Luke 24:46,47; Romans 1:5; Galatians 3:29; Revelation 5:9

OVERVIEW

God is wonderfully breaking into people groups worldwide. His blessing of every people is a theme we see throughout Scripture.

AIMS

In this session, we're not so much interested in conveying information as in generating an emotional response. Your teenagers will, as a result of this session:

- Know some of what God is doing worldwide, and how that fits with the biblical theme of God's blessing the nations;
- Consider where they fit in God's global plan;
- Act by inserting into their prayers a plea for God to bless one of the planet's people groups—whether it's an unreached one or their own.

LESSON COMMENTARY

Don't even think about trying to share all this information with your students. This is background commentary for you as you prepare.

HMMMM?!?

Could God actually use His people to reach every person on earth with the good news of salvation? In the late 1800s, a British military official was asked how long it would take to get a message from Queen Victoria to every person on earth. He scratched his head, pondered the strategies, and replied in all seriousness, "Two years." Today the Coca-Cola Company has very realistic plans to put a Coke in the hand of every person on earth by the year 2000.

If God's people were a bit better clued in to what God has said in His Word about strategy and into what He's doing in our world today, what might our answer be to the question: Can the claims of Christ actually be presented to the world?

The answer is yes. As the gospel penetrates an ethnic group within

a country, new believers can be taught immediately to share the Good News with perhaps two of their relatives and neighbors. Some of those would respond to faith in Christ. And they in turn would be discipled to share with a couple more of their own people.

If that simple strategy were implemented, every person on earth would be personally presented the gospel within just a few years' time.

The key, of course, is penetrating every distinct grouping of people with the gospel and teaching them to duplicate themselves. But that's exactly the strategy God has outlined in Scripture. And, except in the West, it is being implemented in much of the rest of the world:

- The Body of Christ in China grew from about one million in 1949 to as many as 80 to 100 million today.
- Every day another 34,000 are added to the Body in Latin America.
- In Africa, churches are multiplying so rapidly that half the continent's population will claim Jesus Christ as Lord and Savior by the year 2000.
- David Wang of Asia Outreach International says of the revivals and spiritual movements in Asia: "We don't even call it a harvest anymore. We call it 'the great in-gathering.'"

See other encouraging breakthroughs on the "Global Breakthrough" sheet you'll cut apart and hand out to your students.

God is doing something awesome in our world today.

BACK TO THE BIBLE

But then He's always been doing awesome things. A quick sprint through Scripture reveals a theme not often noticed in Christianity that is sometimes only me-centered.

Sometimes we treat the Word as if it were a school yearbook. When you receive your yearbook, whose picture do you look for first? Your own, of course. And unfortunately, that's the way many of us look at the Book: If it's not about me, it's not very interesting. If it doesn't have a good promise or immediate personal application, I won't bother reading further. For example, most of us can quote what we think is the rest of "Be still, and..." from Psalm 46:10, *NIV*. But why do we never hear the actual rest of the verse?

Yes, the Book is about us. But we miss so much when we ignore the fact that it's primarily about Him—about what He is doing in history.

What *is* He doing? He's making strategic breakthroughs into every ethnic group on the earth. And He's deigned to use us ordinary believers, His people, to do it.

Let's glance at the biblical strategy:

- Genesis 12:1-3—God blessed Abraham and promised blessing to all families of the earth;
- Genesis 18:18—God blessed Abraham and promised blessing to all families or peoples of the earth (see note in box);
- Genesis 22:17,18—God again blessed Abraham and promised blessing to all nations of the earth;
- Genesis 26:4—God blessed Isaac and promised blessing to all peoples of the earth;

- Genesis 28:14—God blessed Jacob and promised blessing to all peoples of the earth.

By now it's obvious God wants us to notice this two-part program of blessing:

1. He will bless His people and
2. Through His people He will offer blessing to every unit of humanity on the planet.

Let's look at a few more passages:

- 2 Chronicles 6:32,33—The temple was for all peoples;
- Psalm 67:1,2,7—The passage is startlingly clear: God blesses His people to be a blessing to every people group on the face of the earth:

"God be gracious to us and bless us,

And cause His face to shine upon us—

That Thy way may be known on the earth,

Thy salvation among all nations. . . .

God blesses us,

That all the ends of the earth may fear Him"

(Psalm 67:1,2,7).

- Malachi 1:11—God will accomplish His purpose of blessing every people;
- Matthew 28:19—We are to disciple all the nations (*ethne* in the original Greek, from which we get our English word *ethnic*);
- Luke 2:29-32—Jesus was born as a Light to all people groups (Gentiles) as well as to bless the Jews;
- Luke 24:45-47—Jesus emphasized Scripture's theme that the gospel is to be proclaimed to all nations or people groups;
- Romans 1:5—All the nations are our focus;
- Revelation 5:9—God will accomplish His purpose of blessing every people. Some from every people will be present in eternity.

The basic point is: Throughout the Bible, God's plan is to bless His people and, through them, bless every people on the earth with the offer of redemption in Christ. Their responsibility, then, is to take that Good News to every individual in their society.

PERSONAL POP QUIZ

It's one thing to rattle through a lesson about God's great, global purpose. It's another thing to look in the mirror and ask yourself as a youth worker some serious questions:

- Am I where God wants me?
- Did I make a commitment to some kind of ministry—missions, for example—when I was a child that I need to revisit?
- Even when my own life seems crazy, am I confident of God's solid, controlled purpose in history?

Note: The biblical term "nation" (as used today of the Cherokee nation) is not the same as a country. In the Bible, nations, peoples and families are often used interchangeably, although these terms technically have specific slants of meaning.

It's time to stop thinking political country and start thinking people group when it comes to the Great Commission. For example, within the political boundaries of the country of Mali are several distinct nations or ethnic groups which are separated by strong barriers of language, culture or acceptance.

One of those people groups in the West African country of Mali is—believe it or not—the Bozos. There will, of course, be bozos in heaven. (Fortunately, we'll love everybody then.) But these 70,000 real Bozo people will be represented in heaven—even though there is absolutely no church among them now. God promises that some from every people (see Revelation 5:9) will be there—including the Bozos. Pray for them now.

Note: This overview, naturally, raises many questions—which is why we're hosting *A Sunday for the World*.

The purpose of this Sunday's program is to expand vision and raise curiosity about what God is doing today in the big picture and what our part is in it. With such a huge scope, we're obviously not going to answer every question. (To find out more on these topics, see For Further Study below as well as the Follow-up Action Steps and Resources in the *Sunday for the World* packet.)

- Do I recognize every blessing in my life as having a distinct purpose in the lives of people in every nation?
- Can I quote the remainder of "Be still, and..." (Psalm 46:10, *NIV*) or am I perhaps a bit too focused on myself and what I can get out of God? (Go ahead and check the reference.)
- Do I really think it's possible these teenagers I'm teaching will be guiding the global vision of the church in the year 2020? Or is that one of the reasons I plead with Jesus to return *soon*?

For Further Study

- Read through *Catch the Vision 2000* by Bill and Amy Stearns (Bethany House, 1001). Available at Christian bookstores or call 800-MISSION.
- On your own or with a few friends, work through START, a study of God's global plan and your part in it. Available from Caleb Project, 10 W. Dry Creek Circle, Littleton, CO 80120-4170; Phone: 303-730-4170 Fax: 303-730-4177 Internet e-mail: Info@cproject.com.

LESSON PLAN

PREPARATION

1. Study the Bible passages listed and the material in your Lesson Commentary.
2. Pray that God will help your high school students catch a vision of their places in God's global plan.
3. Think through the following Lesson Plan activities.
4. Prepare materials as listed.

MATERIALS NEEDED

- A Bible for each student;
- A photocopy of the Student Worksheets for each expected student and visitor;
- Photocopy "Breakthrough News"—either make one copy and clip apart the breakthroughs or make enough copies for each of your students plus anticipated visitors (see alternate Focus activity);
- A world map—particularly in the Focus activity (optional);
- Audiocassette player—see the Decide alternate activity (optional).

High School Session

SESSION AT A GLANCE

Focus (10-15 Minutes)
Global Breakthrough Reports
Focus Alternate Activity

Discover (15-20 Minutes)
People-Group Thinking
Discover Alternate Activity

Decide (10 Minutes)
God Is Doing It
Decide Alternate Activity

Do (2 Minutes)
World-Class Special FX

THE SESSION

AS STUDENTS ARRIVE

Greet students by handing each a Student Worksheet 1 and pencil. Encourage them to do the As You Arrive activity by finding the listed countries on the Student Worksheet's world map.

FOCUS (10-15 MINUTES)

This opening activity is designed to hook your students' interest in God's global perspective.

Global Breakthrough Reports

Direct students to jot on their Student Worksheet maps notes from the Breakthrough Reports. You can choose any of several methods to present the breakthroughs:

- Cut apart "Breakthrough News" and pass breakthroughs out as students arrive; ask students to read one or two each. Be sensitive to those who are embarrassed to read in a group;
- Read the breakthroughs yourself as if you're reporting the news;
- Ask a local Christian radio DJ to attend your session and read through the breakthroughs as a radio report;
- Prearrange for three students to sit at a table and ham up their roles as TV news reporters who alternate as they read the breakthroughs;
- Snag early arrivers to step into a side room and record two or three of the breakthroughs on tape cassette, then simply play the tape during this Focus activity while students jot notes on their maps;
- Arrange for a group of students to meet a day or so before *A Sunday for the World* to videotape a newscast using the breakthroughs;

High School Session

• If your church has closed-circuit video facilities, see about arranging a broadcast of the breakthroughs from a central place in your church, with your group and several other groups viewing the broadcast on video monitors.

FOCUS ALTERNATE ACTIVITY (10-15 MINUTES)

If you'd rather, simply photocopy "Breakthrough News" as it is for each student. As students arrive, hand the sheets out along with the Student Worksheet. Tell each student **Browse through these reports and pick out the ones you find most interesting.** As you begin your session, ask for responses. Add your own choices of most interesting items. Conclude this opening activity by praying that God would continue to reveal Himself throughout the world, and that we might be part of that great process in our day.

DISCOVER (15-20 MINUTES)

This section of the lesson guides students to discover the basic pattern of God's global plan as revealed in Scripture.

People-Group Thinking

Divide your group into small teams of three or four each. Distribute Student Worksheet 2. Assign to each team Study 1, 2 or 3. In a large class, feel free to have several teams working on Study 1, several more on 2, etc. As a quick team finishes its study, direct them to go on to the other study sections.

Team Study 1: Get a Clue

Genesis 12:1-3 (Who's God talking to here?)

Genesis 18:18

Genesis 22:17,18

Genesis 26:4 (Who's God talking to here?)

Genesis 28:14 (Who's God talking to here?)

God repeats a two-part promise five times. The promise is:

1. To...(bless Abraham—and Isaac and Jacob—and their descendants...)
2. And through him/them to... (bless every family/people/nation).

Galatians 3:29

Who are Abraham's descendants? (All believers)

Team Study 2: Blessed to Bless

Psalm 67:1,2

Psalm 67:7

Why does God bless us? (That His way and salvation would be known by all nations.)

God's program is to:

1. bless His people and
2. for His people to bless (every nation or people).

Psalm 46:10

Which is more popular to most Christians—the first half or second half of this verse? Why? (The first half. It's natural to be more interested in ourselves. Being interested in others—especially those of other races—is supernatural. A supernatural desire to bless others is one of the special effects God displays in our lives as we honestly follow Him.)

Team Study 3: The Final Frontier

Matthew 28:19

Who are we commanded to disciple? (The nations.)

Luke 24:46,47

In Jesus' definition of the gospel, what two-word phrase from Matthew 19:28 is repeated? (All nations.)

Revelation 5:9

There are maybe 24,000 people groups (the biblical term "nations") today in about 230 countries. How many of these people groups will be represented by at least some individuals in heaven? (All.)

Conclude this Discover section by asking **Out of the 24,000 people groups today, how many do you think don't yet have the gospel?** (Don't bother being technical, but technically about 10,000 peoples grouped in about 2,000 clusters do not yet have an effective church movement. A simple response is: About 2,000. Only 500 to 600 of the 10,000 have no Christian work going on among them—yet. But we know they will be presented the gospel since they'll have representatives in heaven. It's only a matter of when and through whom.)

DISCOVER ALTERNATE ACTIVITY (15-20 MINUTES)

The Great Debate

Older high schoolers especially can zip through the simple studies listed above. So feel free to complicate their lives with this activity. As above, break students into teams and allow just seven to eight minutes to work through Study 1, 2 or 3.

Assign another team the task of being devil's advocate by preparing—through some misapplication of logic, through misuse of Scripture or in any possible way—to promote the following false ideas. Allow them the seven to eight minutes as well to prepare. (Cut out the following items for your devil's advocates.)

- Point A: The Old Testament described the way God operated in Old Testament times. So His plan revealed to Abraham, Isaac and Jacob doesn't have anything to do with us today.
- Point B: Everyone knows that the point of Christianity is to be all we can be and to live a really nice life. My Christianity has nothing to do with someone off in Bunga-Bunga Land.
- Point C: We can't save the world, and it's getting to be a darker and darker place. So the smartest thing to do is defend ourselves and our families from the attacks of evil and hope Jesus comes back really soon.

Allow just 10 to 12 minutes for The Great Debate. Have a study team present its findings in a two-minute period. Then allow the devil's advocate team one minute to counter that presentation with its arguments. Point A attacks the findings of Study 1. Point B attacks the findings of Study 2. Point C attacks the findings of Study 3.

After each devil's advocate argument, direct the study team to counter with a rebuttal statement that discounts that attack.

Statements for each team might be:

Team Study 1: Get a Clue—We believers today are the descendants (see Galatians 3:29) who will bless the nations as stated in the Genesis passages.

Team Study 2: Blessed to Bless—The Bible is clear (see Psalm 67:1,2) that the purpose of God's blessing on us is for others of all nations, not just so we'll have nicer lives.

Team Study 3: The Final Frontier—Jesus commanded us to move out to disciple nations, not to stay home and build fortresses because we're afraid of the big, bad world.

DECIDE (10 MINUTES)

This activity helps your students generally begin applying the aims of the lesson.

God Is Doing It

Let your high schoolers enjoy something that comes only rarely to them: a good story. Just don't tell them you're going to tell them a story; they'll have to roll their eyes as if a story is beneath them. Just jump right in. Read the story or have a very good student reader present it. Obviously if you can tell it from memory with dramatic effect, it'll have more impact.

A few years ago in a country in southern Africa we'll say is Tanzania, a South African man we'll call Clarence trekked into the region of the Yao (yah-ow) people. That isn't the real country, and Clarence isn't really his name. But because he wants to go back into this country again to the Yao people, for security reasons we'll have to use fake names. But it is a true story, okay?

Clarence entered a Yao village and asked for a meeting with the headmen to get permission to build a home. The chief and elders served him tea, then asked him his name. "Che"—which means mister—"Clarence." The chief and elders looked around at each other wide-eyed. The chief asked, "And why have you come?" Clarence said, "I have come to tell your people about Isa Al Masih"—Jesus the Messiah. The men looked startled again, then quickly agreed, "Yes, you may build your house here."

Several months later, Clarence was finishing a section of his roof when the chief strolled by. "Do you know why we let you stay in the village?" the chief asked. Clarence shrugged. The chief went on: "Because twenty-one years ago an old black man came over the hill and asked to meet with us as you did. After tea we asked him his name, and he said, 'Che Clarence'—which is not an African name at all. When we asked him why he had come, he said, 'I have

come to tell your people about Isa Al Masih'—your exact words. We allowed him to stay, and soon four of our people became Christians. We ran them out of the village. And we murdered Che Clarence. Now, twenty-one years later, you with your pale skin come and say the exact words Che Clarence did. We let you stay because we thought you were his ghost."

So Clarence knew God had him living among the Yao for a very specific purpose. And soon so many Yao began responding to the gospel that the Muslim authorities took notice. One January morning, Clarence looked out to see a long line of 24 Muslim priests or imams walking toward his house. The entire village followed. Something was definitely up.

The head imam said, "We have come to ask you some questions about your Christianity." Clarence said, "That will be fine. But let us first send away the people. I will send away the Christians, and you send away the Muslims." The imam agreed, and the leaders squeezed into the house and sat on the floor. After tea, Clarence began, "To show that my answers come from God, I will try to answer each question from the Word of God." And he passed out Bibles to each of the 24 imams.

The head imam presented the first question: "Why do you Christians say there are three Gods—the Father, the Son and the Mother?"

Clarence told the group the page number for Deuteronomy 6:4: "Hear, O Israel! The Lord is our God, the Lord is one! And you shall love the Lord your God with all your heart and with all your soul and with all your might." Then Clarence did the best he could to explain that Christians worship the one true God as the Father, Son and Spirit.

The questioning went on until noon, when the imams stood and filed out to do their noon prayers. Then they returned, sat down and the grilling went on through the afternoon. At several points, Clarence stood and paced back and forth, waving his hands to describe difficult points. Promptly at 5 P.M., the Muslim priests stood and strode from the house. The last to leave was the head imam. He said to Clarence, "I am Sheik Abu Bakr. Come to my house in the city next week." Then he too left briskly.

A week later, Clarence visited the sheik. After tea and the required small talk, the sheik said, "Do you know why we came to your house last week?"

"Yes," said Clarence. "To ask questions about Christianity."

"No. We came to kill you." Now, an African never admits he wants to harm you for fear that the spirits will harm him. Clarence sat back as the sheik continued: "For three days we worked our magic, and brought our potions and medicines in the pockets of our robes. We sat in an arrangement in your house so that our power would focus on you. You were to be struck dumb, and the people would laugh at you as a foolish Christian who couldn't even answer a question. But you talked and talked. Then you were to be paralyzed and finally fall over dead. But what did you do? You stood and walked back and forth and waved your hands and talked all day. We knew the Spirit you had was more powerful than our

spirits and our best magic. And now I want to become a Christian."

Clarence was now totally stunned. "Uh, why would you say that?"

"When I was a boy," the sheik said, "I lived in a village near the mountains. One evening I went up on the mountainside and suddenly there was a blazing light. I thought it was a fire, and I crept closer. Then a book appeared out of the light and a voice told me, 'Read.' I was frightened, and I said, 'I cannot read.' But the voice said again, 'Read.' And I looked at the book, and I could read. Then the book disappeared and the light was gone. I ran all the way down the mountainside to the village, and everyone was asking me what the fire was. I finally told them what had happened, and they all laughed: 'You cannot read. You have not learned.' Then someone brought a book, and I read it to all the village. The Muslims heard about this, and they took me to their finest schools, and for fifteen years I have been the chief debater of Christians in all of southern Africa."

Clarence was trying to take all this in. "But why do you now want to become a Christian?"

"Because," said Sheik Abu Bakr, "you may remember the first question I asked you."

"Yes, it was about the Trinity and we turned to 'Hear, O Israel! The Lord is our God, the Lord is one! And you shall love the Lord your God with all your heart and with all your soul and with all your might.'"

"Yes," replied the sheik. "And when I was a boy, that was the verse I read in the book on the mountain."

Clarence was shocked, then irritated. "But wait a minute. If you knew then that the Bible is the true Word of God, why did you keep asking me and asking me those difficult question all day long?"

The sheik smiled. "The other imams with me are the Muslim leaders of the entire country. And I wanted them to hear for themselves the truth from God's Word. And now I want to become a Christian."

Let's pray for this man upon whom God obviously has His hand. (Lead the group in prayer for the sheik, for the Yao people, and for the missionary we've called Clarence as he raises up a team to go back to this people group where God is doing wonderful things for the sake of His name.)

DECIDE ALTERNATE ACTIVITY (10 MINUTES)

If you have a mature class, sit among your students to assure them they have equal time to express their opinions and toss out the following discussion questions: So what? What does any of this have to do with you? Any comments?

DO (2 MINUTES)

This closing activity allows students to express, if only mentally, a step of commitment to God's global plan.

World-Class Special FX

Simply read through the text on the Student Worksheet under this heading and allow students to pray silently after you.

Point out the final action step of finding people to pray, and offer to be one of those people for any of your students. Suggest you'll be available right after class to sign on to a student's prayer team. Also remind them to make sure whoever they live with gets a Family Activity Guide. It's got some cool tidbits for high schoolers.

STUDENT WORKSHEET 1

AS YOU ARRIVE

How's your global geography? Mull over the map below and label the following countries and cities:

- Ecuador
- Puerto Rico
- Finland
- Moscow
- Frankfurt
- Somalia
- New Delhi
- Myanmar (Burma)
- Mongolia
- Seoul
- The Philippines
- Sydney
- Bucksnort, Tennessee

GLOBAL BREAKTHROUGHS

God is doing some special demos of His power across the world today. Jot some notes on the reports that interest you. Try to pinpoint the location of the incident on this map.

STUDENT WORKSHEET 2

PEOPLE-GROUP THINKING

As a group, look up the references and answer the questions. Be prepared to share your answers with the whole group. (Hint: The words *families*, *peoples* and *nations* in the Bible refer to ethnic groups or people groups, not necessarily political countries. For example, the Kurds are a people group even though they have no country. Got it?)

Team Study 1: Get a Clue

Genesis 12:1-3 (Who's God talking to here?)

Genesis 18:18

Genesis 22:17,18

Genesis 26:4 (Who's God talking to here?)

Genesis 28:14 (Who's God talking to here?)

God repeats a two-part promise five times. The promise is:

    1. To

    2. And through him/them to

Galatians 3:29

Who are Abraham's descendants?

Team Study 2: Blessed to Bless

Psalm 67:1,2

Psalm 67:7

Why does God bless us?

God's program is to:

    1. bless us His people and

    2. for us to bless

Psalm 46:10

Which is more popular to most Christians—the first half or second half of this verse? Why?

Team Study 3: The Final Frontier

Matthew 28:19

Who are we commanded to disciple?

Luke 24:46,47

In Jesus' definition of the gospel, what two-word phrase from Matthew 19:28 is repeated?

Revelation 5:9

There are maybe 24,000 people groups (the biblical term "nations") today in about 230 countries. How many of these people groups will be represented by at least some individuals in heaven?

GOD IS DOING IT

When Christians start thinking they're the ones who need to save the world, to get all the people groups to heaven, they get weird. They start pointing long, bony fingers of blame to try to motivate us through guilt. They start whining for more money to solve all the world's needs. There's nothing wrong with challenges and funding appeals, but these things are sometimes misguided attempts to do what only God can do. He's the One who's taking people from every tribe, tongue and nation to heaven. We need to let Him do His work. And we do that through our obedience—constantly asking for cleansing from sin and constantly saying to Him, "Whatever—I'll do it." We obey; He does the saving-the-world bit.

Relax and enjoy a recent, true story that points out God's supernatural power to bring Good News to every nation through our personal obedience.

WORLD-CLASS SPECIAL FX

Tired of a Christianity that is basically:

1. going to lots of meetings and
2. being nice?

Get global. Think big. Your life will take on special effects (like adventure, challenge, the need for real courage, the rush of bringing people to heaven, knowing what's really going on in the world, etc., etc.) when you find your part in God's global plan. That part might be here or wherever. Are you willing to let God work through you? No matter where? No matter what?

_____ I don't want to say "Anything and anywhere" to God right now. I just want to keep coming to meetings and trying to be a nice person. Or at least acting like I'm a nice person. I'll plan to miss out on the adventure of why God is leaving me on this planet till my next level of life in heaven. Or maybe just till I'm old and can't do anything really adventurous anyway.

_____ I'm ready to move out to obey God no matter what and no matter where. I'll ask some wizened old person like a parent or teacher to pray for me in this commitment. And I'll expect some special effects in my life soon.

If it's what you want to pray today, repeat silently in your head as your teacher closes with this prayer:

Dear God,

Thanks for being a global God—and for asking me to be part of what you're doing. —Help me find my part—in your worldwide plan. —If you want me here, I'll do it. —If you want me some-place else on the planet, —I'll go. —For the sake of Your name, — Amen.

A *Sunday for the World* Action Step

If you prayed that prayer above, make it *today* that you find somebody or several some-bodies who will regularly pray for you in this commitment. Also, make sure you and who-ever you live with gets a Family Activity Guide. It's got more stuff on your part in God's global plan.

SPRINT THROUGH THE BIBLE

KEY VERSE

"Behold, I say to you, lift up your eyes, and look on the fields, that they are white for harvest." John 4:35

KEY BIBLE PASSAGES

Genesis 12:1-3; 18:18; 22:17,18; 26:4; 28:14,15; Psalm 67:1,2,7; 105:1; 145:4,10-12; Proverbs 25:25; Isaiah 12:4,5; Habakkuk 1:5; Malachi 1:11; Matthew 24:14; 28:19,20; Luke 24:46,47; John 4:35; 2 Timothy 2:15; Revelation 5:9; 12:9

OVERVIEW

This session for college and adult classes emphasizes that God is doing wonderful things globally. We can better understand His work today by recognizing two principles:

- People-group thinking;
- Being blessed to bless every people.

This is an extremely fast-paced lesson spanning input from Genesis to Revelation. The point is overall impact, not the digestion of detailed information. So the clock will, as usual, be your enemy during the lesson. When those getting hooked on the topics presented want to slow down to discuss and analyze, suggest that there will be time for those luxuries in future studies of the big picture of what God is doing. For now, keep moving briskly.

AIMS

By the end of this session, your participants will:

1. Realize God is moving in wonderful ways across the globe.
2. Understand the principles that God reaches individuals within people groups, and that God's people are blessed to be a blessing to every one of these people groups.
3. Feel curious to find out more about what God is doing in the big picture. If your fellowship is offering follow-up Bible study courses such as *Destination 2000* or *Catch the Vision 2000*, be prepared to give a solid plug at the close of this session for interested participants to sign up for the course.

LESSON COMMENTARY

LOOK WHAT GOD IS DOING

Review some of the "Breakthroughs in God's Global Plan" at the end of this lesson. Such good news is refreshing to many discouraged

Adult Session

THE TWO-THIRDS WORLD

Often the "third world" is used to describe the developing countries of the world. During the Cold War era, Westerners considered themselves, of course, the "first world." Communists with their powerful threats were the second. And everyone else was, well, just third.

Actually, developing countries have two-thirds of the world's population and live on two-thirds of the earth's surface. And believers from the Two-Thirds World now make up more than two-thirds of the Body of Christ. They're actually the majority of Christians.

Wouldn't it help adjust our worldview if we began referring to the Two-Thirds World? Maybe we in the West will begin to realize we're only the "One-Third World."

believers who secretly believe we're losing.

"Like cold water to a weary soul, so is good news from a distant land" (Proverbs 25:25).

Why don't we hear more positive news about what God is doing?

- In the Sunday service of *A Sunday for the World*, we'll see that North American believers are now just a very small (actually about 10 percent) of the world's committed believers. And most of what's happening in the Body of Christ is out there in the majority 90 percent, mostly in the Two-Thirds World.

- We don't have very good communication links with the Body of Christ in the Two-Thirds World, where the gospel is spreading like wildfire. Also, Satan thinks his job is to "deceive the whole world" (Revelation 12:9). So he makes sure we only hear select, bad news about what's going on in the world. He just doesn't like us to hear any good news about spiritual victories abroad; we might actually get encouraged enough to seriously join in.

- We are to "make known His deeds among the peoples; make them remember that His name is exalted.... For He has done excellent things; let this be known throughout the earth" (Isaiah 12:4,5). Other passages command us or describe our natural tendency to brag about God's works:

"Your saints will extol you. They will tell of the glory of your kingdom and speak of your might, so that all men might know of your mighty acts" (Psalm 145:10-12, NIV).

"One generation will commend your works to another; they will tell of your mighty acts" (Psalm 145:4, NIV).

"Oh give thanks to the Lord, call upon His name; make known His deeds among the peoples" (Psalm 105:1).

Maybe we don't share the Good News often enough.

A SPRINT THROUGH THE BIBLE

Often we look at the Bible as if it's a school yearbook; we focus on photos of our own faces, then on those close to us. If the Word doesn't have something specific for me right now, it seems boring. But this Book is about Him and His life—not just about me. Seeing the big picture of what God is saying throughout the Word is crucial to finding out where I fit in His great plan.

The following passages provide a bit of a glimpse into that theme of Scripture. Recurring factors in God's global plan are:

- People-group thinking—God deals with individuals, but not necessarily individuals alienated from everyone else. There is a constant reminder that God deals with individuals within the context of people groups (seen in terms such as families, nations, etc.).

- Blessed to be a blessing—God blesses His own people in order to bless every earthly people group.

Your upcoming session during *A Sunday for the World* features A Sprint Through the Bible covering the following passages and concepts:

- Genesis 12:1-3; 18:18; 22:17,18; 26:4; 28:14

Notes: Abraham, probably an Assyrian, was chosen by God to start a new people—God's people.

God promised repeatedly to bless him and through him and his offspring to bless every people, nation or family on earth.

Often a group is surprised to learn that the first phrase of Genesis 28:15 in the Septuagint, the Greek version of the Old Testament from which Jesus frequently quoted, reads, "And, lo, I am with you always"—which should sound pretty familiar.

• Psalm 67:1,2,7

Notes: We often cut the sentence of Psalm 67:1,2 in half: We want to hear about God blessing us, but we tend to ignore the idea that the purpose for that blessing is for the sake of others.

Here again we see the term *nation*. A nation in the Bible isn't so much a political country as it is a people, a distinct cultural family. Later, the Jews begin to call all the nations or peoples besides themselves the Gentiles.

Verse 7, as the final sentence in this Hebrew poem, circles back to the emphasis of the poem's first lines. Thus the best translation uses "that" between the clauses to emphasize a cause and effect—"God blesses us, *that* all the ends of the earth may fear Him."

• Malachi 1:11; Matthew 28:19,20; Luke 24:46,47

Notes: The word *nation* in this passage is, in the original Greek of the New Testament *ethne*, from which we get our English word *ethnic*. Jesus told us to disciple—"make follower-learners"—of every distinct ethnic group on the face of the earth.

That familiar "Lo, I am with you always" is, again, from Genesis 28:15. This is no new commandment Jesus has given. It's the same basic Great Commission God has mandated all along: I will bless you/all authority is given to me, and you will be a blessing to every people/make disciples of every people.

• Revelation 5:9

Note: Every people group will have representatives around the throne. That's how we know that some of the Bosnian nation will respond to the gospel. It's just a matter of when and through whom.

• Matthew 24:14

Note: Without getting controversial as to possible prophetic interpretations of this verse, it simply says that there will be an end to God's global plan of offering His blessing to every people on earth.

INTEREST TO ACTION

Some of the study we're doing in *A Sunday for the World* will leave some participants eager to move into action. They might have heard of the idea of adopting one of the remaining unreached people groups of the world, and they want to do that now. They may call for a special week of prayer for the world. They may announce they're now heading for Mongolia. But leaping from interest straight to action, although characteristic of the North American personality, can be dangerous.

Zeal without knowledge can lead to mistakes in outreach. Good

intentions in prayer don't necessarily mean we know what to ask or what is on God's heart, so our prayer energy fizzles when answers don't come. Trying to adopt an unreached people without a clue as to the hows and whys of such a move can cause confusion in a fellowship.

So be patient with your participants in this upcoming Bible study. They may respond enthusiastically to the message of the session. But they need to be cautioned to move from catching that vision of God's heart for every people to the next stage of building that vision—not to the next stage, jumping into action without preparation—yet.

Encourage them to study first—studying God's world—the harvest field, studying God's work—His strategies in today's harvest force, and most of all studying God's Word:

"Be diligent to present yourself approved to God as a workman who does not need to be ashamed, handling accurately the word of truth"
(2 Timothy 2:15).

LESSON PLAN

1. Carefully study this session's Bible passages and read through the Lesson Commentary.
2. Pray that your study group will know, feel and act on the objectives for the session.
3. Prepare materials and equipment as listed below.

MATERIALS NEEDED

- Bibles;
- Photocopies of the Student Worksheet for each person;
- Cut apart slips of "Breakthroughs in God's Global Plan." (Optional: Consider photocopying the sheet before you cut it up. Pass out the cut-up slips as suggested below; then pass out the entire "Breakthroughs in God's Global Plan" at the close of the session.);
- A map or globe for simple reference (optional);
- Overhead transparency of Sprint Through the Bible passages by photocopying them onto an acetate sheet (optional);
- Overhead projector, white board, chalkboard or flipchart and appropriate markers (optional).

SESSION AT A GLANCE

Focus (15-25 Minutes)
Opening Prayer
World News

Discover (15-20 Minutes)
Sprint Through the Bible

Decide (10 Minutes)
Discussion: So What?

Do (1-2 Minutes)
The Closing Prayer for the Peoples

THE SESSION

FOCUS (15-25 MINUTES)

The purpose of these opening activities is not information or education. Especially the breakthroughs section is simply designed for impact: "I'm surprised at what God is doing. This is interesting." So be ruthless in urging class members to jump in quickly with their breakthroughs. Or, if delivering the breakthroughs yourself, be staccato in your pacing. This is not a class lecture period where you expect listeners to remember much. You're looking for an emotional response.

Before the Session

As early comers arrive, pass out the cut-up slips of breakthroughs. Ask each if he or she would like to read a short item or two. Relieve any non-readers or slow readers from being embarrassed and thinking they must read.

Alternate: Don't pass out the slips of breakthroughs before the session. Plan instead to present with a friend a sort of newscast of these breakthroughs.

Write on the chalkboard: "What significant events might God accomplish during the rest of your lifetime?" As participants arrive, encourage them to think through the question. Encourage them to be as serious or frivolous as they want. Be prepared with some suggestions of what global events could yet happen during your lifetime:

- Canada and the U.S. merge;
- Indestructible mattress carrier handles are invented;
- Elvis is discovered alive and well and living in Tibet;
- Every last culture has its own church.

Opening Prayer

"I DON'T BELIEVE THIS STUFF"

Invariably, you'll have skeptics say they don't believe what they're hearing. If so:

- Recite Habakkuk 1:5: "Look among the nations! Observe! Be astonished! Wonder! Because I am doing something in your days—you would not believe if you were told."
- Encourage him or her to find someone with a computer and modem and e-mail a request to world.christian@gen.org for all the documentation for these items—and hundreds more breakthrough reports as well.

World News

Begin your session by calling for current events. **From what we know from newspapers, magazines, radio and TV, what's happening in the world today?** Jot key words of responses on your overhead/board or flipchart. Ask **How many of these items have much to do with what's happening spiritually in our world?**

Undoubtedly few or none of the news items will have anything to do with spiritual breakthroughs. And most world news items are bad news. That makes us want to simply focus on our own lives, where hopefully we can at least try to handle things.

Once you are certain the slips of breakthroughs are passed out, refer briefly (20 seconds) to John 4:35, "Behold, I say to you, lift up your eyes, and look on the fields."

Suggest that sometimes we're so intent on our walk in following Him, on our own next personal step, that He must tell us to lift up our eyes and look around.

Distribute Student Worksheets. Then call for volunteers to randomly stand and read the breakthrough items about what God is doing around the world. If you prefer, you might simply read items yourself.

Very briefly refer to maps when helpful. (Note: If you or your coteacher don't readily know where to point on a map, don't spend any time perusing the globe. The "Uhhhh..., I think it's right here....; no, maybe...." is extremely boring to other participants.)

Watch your time carefully on this activity. You might need to cut off the reports; as when hosting a good party, cut it off while they're asking for more. (If you photocopy the entire list of breakthroughs for your participants, they'll be able to read later what wasn't reported in the session.)

Alternate Activity: With a friend, present a sort of news desk review of the breakthroughs, quickly taking turns at reading each item in a broadcast style.

DISCOVER (15-20 MINUTES)

The point of this blitz is not in-depth Bible study. The objective is to impress participants that we need to look more carefully at the Book as a unified, cohesive revelation of God's colossal plan of history in which He reaches individuals within distinct groups—peoples or nations. Careful study can come at later study sessions.

Sprint Through the Bible

A good transition to this activity is to state something like: **What God is doing globally today isn't anything new. He's been doing it all along. Let's look into the Word to see that pattern.**

To keep participants participating, challenge the group to look up a reference as you call it out. The first one finding it is to stand and with some good volume read it. An assistant at the overhead projector or chalkboard may uncover or list the references as you announce them.

References include:
Genesis 12:1-3;
Genesis 18:18;
Genesis 22:17,18;
Genesis 26:4;
Genesis 28:14;
Psalm 67:1,2;
Psalm 67:7;
Malachi 1:11;
Matthew 24:14;
Matthew 28:19,20;
Luke 24:46,47;
Revelation 5:9.

Comment *briefly* at various points—not necessarily at each reference—using input from the Lesson Commentary and your own study. Be sure to emphasize:

- As God's people are blessed to bless every people, "every people" includes *our own*.
- We are not just encouraged to bless others. That emphasis is good, but usually leaves us blessing only those we come in contact with—which usually means they're only of our own people group. We are also to purposely reach across cultural barriers to bless individuals in *every* people group.

Alternate Activity: Team Reports. Break up your class into four small teams and assign three of the passages to each. The teams are to read through their assigned passages and be prepared to report what each has to do with:

- Seeing mankind in distinct groups and/or
- Being blessed in order to bless.

Allow just five or six minutes for the teams' reading and discussion. Then ask for quick reports, adding comments from the Lesson Commentary and your own study. Emphasize:

- As God's people are blessed to bless every people, every people includes our own.
- We're not just encouraged to bless others. That emphasis is good, but usually leaves us blessing only those we come in contact with—which usually means they're only of our own people group. We're also to purposely reach across cultural barriers to bless individuals in every people group.

DECIDE (10 MINUTES)

Since the overall session is designed to open up some thinking rather than state conclusions, this discussion period simply allows your group to articulate their opinions and questions about the previous half hour of input. If you use the optional video, seeing the faces of the unreached for a few minutes reminds your group that we're talking about real people with eternal destinies.

Discussion: So What?

Allow your group members to express themselves in comments, opinions and questions. Don't feel you need to answer questions, and avoid coaching the group toward conclusions.

Simply introduce this activity by asking **So what? What do you think about what we've covered today? What are your questions and comments?**

Expect some of the following:

- Why don't we hear more of this?
- I don't believe these news bits.
- Why bother with all the world when we have such needs right here?
- I'd like to study these passages.
- I don't understand this "people group" thing.
- Can we spend more time on this topic sometime?

DO (1-2 MINUTES)

This closing activity encourages participants to the next step of their parts in God's global plan: finding out more.

The Next Step

Close your presentation with a simple question: **What's next?**

What is the next step? Learning more about what God is doing in our era, and what He's been doing all along to bless every people, tribe, tongue and nation on earth—including our own.

If your fellowship will offer a follow-up Bible study of *Catch the Vision 2000, Destination 2000* or another course about our part in God's global plan, give details of when, where and how the course will be offered. If the course is to be offered on an elective basis, have sign-up slips available at the close of the session.

If a course is not to be offered, encourage individuals to further their own studies in *Catch the Vision 2000* (Bethany House), available through your local Christian bookstore.

Closing Prayer

Pray that each member of your class will clarify his or her part in God's global plan—wherever and however God may continue to lead.

Alternate: Suggest that one key way to bless the nations is through prayer. Lead your class in intercession for a particular people group such as the Agul people of southern Russia, the Sudanese people of Indonesia or the Deccani people of India. Even without knowing much about these unreached people groups, we can pray that God will break through the spiritual darkness over them—that God will bless them with the knowledge of salvation in Jesus Christ.

STUDENT WORKSHEET

WORLD NEWS

What does the media have to say about the state of the world today? What's happening in God's domain that the news doesn't seem to mention? Jot notes on these breakthroughs.

SPRINT THROUGH THE BIBLE

List the references given for an on-your-own study later.

SO WHAT?

Without trying to reach earth-shaking conclusions about the input of this session, what comments and questions come to mind? Share briefly your thoughts with the rest of the group.

THE NEXT STEP

I will:

_____ Study more on this topic of God's global plan and my part in it.
_____ Pray this week for one of the world's unreached people groups.

BREAKTHROUGHS IN GOD'S GLOBAL PLAN

- Worldwide: Last year alone, about 120,000,000 people were presented the gospel for the first time.

- The Body of Christ now owns 158,725,000 computers worldwide. Are we using them to link us up for the Kingdom?

- Worldwide: About 1.7 billion people now listen to Christian radio or watch Christian TV on a monthly basis.

- Worldwide: Christians now spend 388,000,000,000 man-hours every year proclaiming the gospel in evangelism.

- Worldwide: David Bryant, an experienced world-watcher with Concerts of Prayer Intl., says, "The landscape of the Church today leaves no question in the minds of many leaders that the Body of Christ is poised at the threshold of a coming world revival.... God is raising up in the Body worldwide a prayer movement that is unprecedented in the history of the Church."

- Worldwide: Two hundred thousand new missionaries by the year 2000? Most believers would say, "Impossible." But even at the present rate of new career mission recruits, the Body of Christ worldwide will send out another 100,000 new missionaries by A.D. 2000—mostly from the Two-Thirds World. How many new missionaries could our congregation send by the year 2000?

- Worldwide: Of all the 24,000 people groups on the face of the earth, possibly only 500-600 are totally unpenetrated by the gospel.

- Worldwide: 85 million copies of the *New International Version* of the Bible have been sold in the past 15 years; and 42 percent of its purchasers say they read the Bible every day.

- Latin America: More than 34,000 a day are added to the Body of Christ across Latin America.

- El Salvador: More than 100,000 believers marched through the streets of San Salvador during a recent "March for Jesus."

- Peru: The 10,000 evangelical churches of this desperate country (unemployment-50 percent) are seeking to plant another 40,000 new churches by the year 2003.

- Brazil: One new church that is just 16 years old now runs 14 Christian radio stations, four TV stations, has missionaries serving in 25 countries and six million members.

- Guatemala: Believers in this country have sent a construction team to build homes for the poor...in Minneapolis, Minnesota.

- Sudan: Thousands of believers have been starved or outright slaughtered for their faith in Christ in this Muslim-ruled country. Most of these sufferers are believers. Yet according to a spokesman for the relief organizations working in this tragic area, "The expansion of the church in Sudan probably is greater than in any other place in the world." When surveyed for what Christians worldwide can do about their situation, Sudan believers repeatedly answered, "Pray for us. Tell many brothers and sisters around the world to pray for us."

- Sudan: A team showing the *Jesus* film in southern Sudan got permission from a large city's local security officials to provide showings to villages in the area. In the midst of strong Muslim influence, 50 showings in one month drew 119,550 viewers. The team reports 87,000 were brought to faith in Christ.

- Chad: Recently in a northern desert village of this parched Muslim country, a missionary and a team of Chadian students explained the gospel to a Muslim crowd. Suddenly a villager began shouting, "Today is the day of grace. Today is the day. We have prayed that

this message would come to us. God has heard us. Now is the time for our decision." And without hesitation 56 Muslims responded to God's call of salvation.

- Africa: More than 20,000 daily are added to the Body of Christ throughout Africa.

- Lebanon: "After the rubble of 17 years of war, the church is expanding like a blooming flower in Lebanon," says a Christian worker. Arab believers from six countries recently mounted intensive evangelism outreaches in Beirut, in Tripoli, in Libya, in Tyre and Sidon. One experienced missionary said he had never seen Muslims so prepared by God to hear, receive and gladly accept without debate the claims of Christ.

- India: Mission India is only one of the church-planting groups reaping a harvest these days in India. The organization offers a training program whose graduates started 18,963 new house churches within a two-year period.

- Mongolia: The young Mongolian church—born in 1991—had by 1994 already sent out its first two missionaries.

- Korea: The number of Korean Protestant missionaries mushroomed from 321 in 1982 to 2,576 in 1992. Today, six new churches open every day in South Korea, and it is site of nine of the world's largest churches—some with more than 800,000 members.

- Korea: On May 25, 1995, the South Korean Church dedicated 105,000 young people for at least two years of mission service. Another 3,000 Korean missionaries are now being trained to go into China.

- Korea: The largest face-to-face meeting of humans in all of history occurred in Seoul when 2.7 million believers gathered for a prayer and mobilization meeting.

- The Philippines: In October 1993, the Philippines was solemnly consecrated to Jesus Christ in a massive rally around the Quirino Grandstand in Luneta Park in Manila—a rally attended by a million believers.

- United States of America: About 85 percent of this country's churches are either stagnant or dying.

- North America: For the first time in 50 years the number of American career missionaries is dropping. For example, the number went from 50,500 in 1988 to 41,142 in 1992. Veteran missionaries who went out after World War II are retiring now in droves, and they're not being replaced. At the same time, the number of North American short-term missionaries has skyrocketed to match the number of North American career missionaries.

- North America: Something is happening in North America. Hundreds of thousands of men are committing themselves to the disciplines of discipleship in Christ at the Promise Keepers conferences. Millions of youth gather to pray around their school flagpoles each September in the grass-roots See You At the Pole prayer movement. More than two million across the U.S. and Canada pray daily for world evangelization.

- North America: Many cities are experiencing a fresh spiritual awakening—mostly among young people. For example, recently in Wichita, Kansas, each of 3000 Christian high schoolers committed themselves to pray over the lockers of 10 students in their schools and to then invite them to a massive rally. Ten thousand showed up at the rally, where more than 6,000 teenagers came to faith in Jesus Christ.

- North America: In spite of the gloom and doom hitting American Christians, every week 34 percent of the American population reads the Bible outside of church. That's 75 million weekly exposed to the Word that "will not return void".

- Worldwide: Every day now the average number added to the Body of Christ worldwide averages 174,000.

- Worldwide: There are now more than 400 Christian research centers established around the globe. And they're finally able to share this kind of information by computer.

HEAVEN IS A WONDERFUL PLACE

OUTLINE

Plan your *A Sunday for the World* service as you would any Sunday service, adjusting if necessary for the 45 minutes needed for the message and its optional learning activities. A suggested schedule might be:

1. Announcements;
2. Opening music and worship;
3. Prayer;
4. Offering;
5. Special music;
6. Message and closing challenge;
7. Participation.

Many people or just a few may be involved in this *A Sunday for the World* service. That is, you may opt to have no special music, a soloist or an entire children's choir. You may choose to have one person present the message, or you might have two or three others join that person to present the "Message Breakthroughs" and to orchestrate the "Skit for the World."

A one-person presentation is easier to plan. A presentation by several offers more interest and variety. Determine the participation as you wish.

THEME

God has a place for each of us in His great global plan that leads us into eternity. That plan and that destiny involve every people group—every culture—on the face of the earth. The process of the plan starts with God blessing us as His people to in turn bless every people—including our own.

KEY VERSE

"You are worthy...because you were slain, and with your blood you purchased men for God from every tribe and language and people and nation." Revelation 5:9, *NIV*

KEY BIBLE PASSAGES

Genesis 1:26,27; 18:18; 22:18; 26:4; Psalm 46:10; 67:1-4,7; 87:2-6; Jeremiah 15:18; Habakkuk 1:5; Matthew 28:19; Luke 13:29; John 2:5; Ephesians 2:10; James 3:9; Revelation 5:9; 21:1-4,10,11,15,16,18,24,26,27; 22:1; 24:1,2

AIMS

Help your fellowship:

- Realize how inextricably our eternal destiny as God's people involves every people on earth—that we're blessed to bless them all.
- Feel encouraged by what God is doing globally, and feel compelled to become more involved.
- Do something to respond to the message—whether to commit to praying for the nations this week, signing up for a Bible study about how to be part of God's global plan or doing both!

MUSIC

Congregational singing and special music can, of course, be on a global theme. Choose congregational songs that are already familiar to your fellowship. Pulling out dusty or oddly unfamiliar "missions" songs only accentuates the idea that God's global plan is only an irregular compartment of the life of the church.

Feel free, however, to use as special music unfamiliar songs that refer to God's global power, presence and plan. For example, a soloist may be able to present the song "God Is in Control." (Background accompaniment tapes for "God Is in Control" are available at your local Christian bookstore or from Star Song Trax from Star Song Communications Inc., P.O. Box 150009, Nashville, TN 37215 U.S.A. TRX 8628.)

THE MESSAGE: HEAVEN IS A WONDERFUL PLACE

Time: 45 minutes

- Does not include optional Pre-Introduction material;
- Includes optional Skit for the World;
- Includes the Bible message and closing challenge.

MATERIALS NEEDED

- Bibles;
- Photocopies of Service Notes sheet;
- Photocopies of Family Activity Guide;
- Photocopies of Prayer Guide;
- Photocopied overheads 1-5 on acetate sheets (optional);
- Overhead projector (pre-check bulb) and screen (optional);
- Large world map or globe (optional).

SPEAKER'S OUTLINE

PRE-INTRODUCTION (IF TIME AVAILABLE)

INTRODUCTION

I. Where We Are Going

   A. Heaven is a real place.

   B. Heaven is a wonderful place.

   C. The heavenly city's inhabitants are from every people.

   D. God keeps a checklist—a registry of the peoples.

   E. Conclusion: Hope you like foreign food!

II. Where We Are Now

   A. In our day God is calling the peoples of the world to Zion.

   B. The pace of what God is doing is accelerating.

   C. He's doing it by blessing us to bless every people.

   D. He has blessed me for a specific role in this historic plan.

   E. Conclusion: My part in God's plan may be small—but it's significant.

CLOSING CHALLENGE

SPEAKER'S NOTES

Feel free to improvise, adjust, edit or add to the following basic outline.

PRE-INTRODUCTION (OPTIONAL)

If you have time, choose from one of the following options to begin hooking your congregation's interest in your message.

Teaser Breakthroughs

Simply share a few breakthroughs from "Message Breakthroughs," some of the good news of what God is doing today. Begin by quoting Habakkuk 1:5:

> "Look among the nations! Observe!
>
> Be astonished! Wonder!
>
> Because I am doing something in your days—
>
> You would not believe if you were told."

Tell a Story

Few approaches enthrall as easily as a good story. This one works very well as a children's story—as well as one for adults. You might simply read the story or you can tell the essential story from memory. Consider calling children down to the front. Assure them and the adults that this is a very recent, very true story. With all your storytelling skills, share the drama:

The Sunday Service

"The Story of the Forbidden Kingdom"

Once in a hidden kingdom far, far into the mountains lived a people ruled by a king with all his pagan religious advisers. Almost no one has ever heard of this kingdom. The king never allowed anyone from the outside to come to the kingdom. It is sometimes called "The Forbidden Kingdom." The people were without God and without hope.

On the lower slopes of the mountains lived a group of young people who began to pray for the Forbidden Kingdom. And, as often happens, one fine spring day they understood that they themselves were the answers to their prayers. The young people gathered provisions and began the long, arduous ascent.

Near the high reaches of the mountains, they came upon the valley of the Imperial City, with the king's palace glistening in the spring sunshine. Suddenly an old man in regal-looking robes stepped from behind a rock and shouted, "You do not belong here!"

The young people prayed silently and answered, "We have come to serve your king and your people in the love of Jesus Christ."

The old man hesitated. "You are not from other countries; you look as we do. I am an elder in the kingdom. You say you want to serve. We shall see. I will take you to the king."

The young people's eyes widened. They prayed silently as they were led to the palace and into the throne room of the king himself. "We have come to serve your people in the love of Jesus Christ," they said.

The king glowered. The elder who ushered in the young people shuffled his feet. "Hmph! We shall see," said the king. He gestured to the guards. "Take them to the rubbish heaps!"

So the young people were led to the trash dumps and ordered to haul the refuse of the townsfolk. They carried rubbish, picked up trash from the streets, and hauled away dead animals from the roads of the kingdom. This they did for seven days. And they sang as they worked.

At the end of the seven days, the king summoned them to appear before him. "So you are here to serve in the love of Jesus Christ," said the king. "We shall see. Take them to work on the walls!"

So the young Christians began to work repairing the walls of the city. They carried rocks from the streams below the palace towers. They mixed clay with straw and water to make bricks. Their hands bled from the rocks. Day after day they were covered with mud and mortar. As the king watched from his palace tower, the young people sang and rebuilt the wall.

After twenty days of making bricks, the young people began to work on the wall. As they did, they looked up to see a solemn line of palace priests in bright yellow robes moving purposefully toward them. The first priest reached the work team and said, "We have come to work with you." The young Christians smiled, sang and worked.

After thirty days the king looked out his palace window to watch the young Christians singing and working alongside the pagan priests. He summoned them to his throne room. "So you have truly come to serve," he said. "It has been reported to me that my priests each evening go to have tea with you so they can learn about the love of this Jesus. I shall offer a proclamation to the people to gather tonight. You may tell them of the love of this Jesus."

That evening the young Christians sang, and for the first time in the ancient history of the hidden kingdom, the people heard of the love of Jesus. Forty of the citizens became followers of Jesus that night.

Soon the young Christians had to return to their own homeland on the slopes of the mountains. As they left the city of the hidden kingdom, the people cried, "Come back to us. And bring others like you!" And just as they lost sight of the city towers on the beginning of their journey home, the young people heard calls behind them. Rushing down the path came the yellow-robed priests. "We have brought you offerings and gifts," the priests called. "So one day soon you may return and bring others like you." Bill and Amy Stearns; *Run With the Vision*, (Minneapolis, Minn.: Bethany House Publishers, 1995) pages 63-65.

Ask at this point: **Wouldn't it be wonderful if the story were true about the Forbidden Kingdom? Well, it *is* true. Let's pray now for that king, for those in the kingdom who indicated they wanted to follow Christ and for the young Christians who are going back soon.** Lead in a short prayer praising God for doing wonderful things in our world today—even in forbidden kingdoms.

INTRODUCTION

God is in control. He knows what He's doing with us and He knows where He's leading us. And that's what today's *Sunday for the World* celebration is all about:

1. Where we are going
2. Where we are now in God's great scheme of things.

I. Where We Are Going

First, let's be clear about where God is leading us. The story of humanity starts in a garden—a garden with the tree of life. But the story ends in a city—the city of the New Jerusalem, sometimes called the City of Zion—with the tree of life.

A. Heaven is a real place.

"And I saw a new heaven and a new earth; for the first heaven and the first earth passed away, and there is no longer any sea.

"And I saw the holy city, new Jerusalem, coming down out of heaven from God, made ready as a bride adorned for her husband.

"And I heard a loud voice from the throne, saying, 'Behold, the tabernacle of God is among men, and He shall dwell among them, and they shall be His people; and God Himself shall be among them,

"And He shall wipe away every tear from their eyes; and there shall no longer be any death; there shall no longer be any mourning or crying, or pain; the first things have passed away'" (Revelation 21:1-4).

- Some of us, like the old prophet Jeremiah, have wounds that are incurable (see Jeremiah 15:18). They may never be cured here and now, but they will be in heaven. Some of us struggle and think we can do no ministry until we are perfect and whole; but we'll never be perfect and whole until heaven. We'll be healed and whole and happy. The old stuff is passed away. The city where we'll live is a wonderful place.

B. Heaven is a wonderful place.

"And he carried me away in the Spirit to a great and high mountain, and showed me the holy city, Jerusalem, coming down out of heaven from God, having the glory of God. Her brilliance was like a very costly stone, as a stone of crystal-clear jasper.

"And the one who spoke with me had a gold measuring rod to measure the city, and its gates and its wall.

"And the city is laid out as a square, and its length is as great as the width; and he measured the city with the rod, fifteen hundred miles; its length and width and height are equal.

"And the material of the wall was jasper; and the city was pure gold, like clear glass" (Revelation 21:10,11,15,16,18).

- The city where Jesus is preparing mansions for us is brilliant, clear as a diamond. And it's a cube 1,500 miles wide, 1,500 miles long, 1,500 miles high! And most Bible scholars feel that there is significance in the fact that the passage doesn't mention where the city settles on the new earth. The repeated phrase "coming down out of heaven" probably means the city never does touch

down but hovers like a huge satellite over the sparkling
new earth. Imagine!

C. The heavenly city's inhabitants are from every people
group, which is the meaning of the biblical word *nation.*

"And the nations shall walk by its light, and the
kings of the earth shall bring their glory into it.

"And they shall bring the glory and the honor
of the nations into it" (Revelation 21:24,26).

"And he showed me a river of the water of life,
clear as crystal, coming from the throne of God and
of the Lamb in the middle of its street. And on
either side of the river was the tree of life, bearing
twelve kinds of fruit, yielding its fruit every month;
and the leaves of the tree were for the healing of the
nations" (Revelation 22:1).

• Who lives in the city? Look back at Revelation 21:27.

"And nothing unclean and no one who practices
abomination and lying, shall ever come into it, but
only those whose names are written in the Lamb's
book of life."

• Is your name going to be written in the book? How about
the names of your family members? Best friends? Is there
any good reason not to invite everybody to the heavenly
party?

• The inhabitants of the city are the billions of us who come
to know Jesus Christ during our earthly lives. And we'll represent every culture on the face of the earth. The Apostle
John actually saw in the future a scene of myriads upon
myriads:

"And they sang a new song: 'You are worthy to take
the scroll and to open its seals, because you were
slain, and with your blood you purchased men for
God from every tribe and language and people and
nation,'" (Revelation 5:9, *NIV*).

• God is interested in individuals, so individual names are
written in this huge book called the Lamb's book of life.
But he is interested in individuals within people groups. Is
every people going to be represented? That's what God says
in Revelation 5:9. And just to make sure every people group

FOR YOUR OWN CONSIDERATION

Every cultural group is represented in heaven. Why?

There is constant reference to
the word *glory* when Scripture
refers to the New Jerusalem. Glory
really only comes from God Himself. So anyone showing glory is
simply reflecting something of the
character of God. As they are
redeemed, they reveal the image
of God that has been invested in
them (see Genesis 1:26,27;
James 3:9).

Scripture says *the nations* bring
their glory into the heavenly city.
So the believers of a nation—let's
say the Cherokee nation—reflect
some aspect of the character of
God in the city. The redeemed of
the Thai people reflect some facet
of God's glory—perhaps His joy—
in a way no other nation can.
Mongolian believers bring into
the city some glory—perhaps the
strength of God's character.

Some from every ethnic group will
be around the throne of the Lamb,
and each *ethnos* will reflect some
aspect of God's character.

In fact, each ethnic group
reflects a different aspect of God's
character. So to get the full picture
of God's glory, of the different
aspects of His character, every *ethnos* needs to be represented in this
city that is illumined by the glory
of God (see Revelation 21:23).

The Sunday Service

is represented in the city, He has another huge book, a registration book listing every people group on the face of the earth.

D. God keeps a checklist—a registry of the peoples.

"The Lord loves the gates of Zion...

"Glorious things are spoken of you, O city of God.

'I shall mention Rahab and Babylon among those who know Me; Behold, Philistia and Tyre with Ethiopia: "This one was born there"'" (Psalm 87:2-4).

• The ones who are born—born again—to live in the city of God forever include some from every people.

The Jews hearing this psalm were probably irritated to find that some of their worst enemies will be living side-by-side with them in the holy city of Zion! "Rahab" stood for Egypt—one of Israel's old oppressors. And there will be some Babylonians in the city—the Babylonians who dragged Jews off to captivity. And some Philistines will be there. Philistines! And some representing the people of Tyre—a center of the most foul Baal worship in Palestine. And some with skin color different than that of the Jews—some from Ethiopia or Cush, which usually referred to all of Africa.

"The Lord shall count when He registers the peoples, 'This one was born there'" (Psalm 87:6).

• God Himself checks off in His great registry of the peoples: "This one and that one" (v. 5) who were born again to live in the City of Zion, the New Jerusalem.

E. Conclusion: Hope you like foreign food!

You like exotic ideas and stories? Then you're going to really love heaven because it's going to be the most culture-packed city in the history of the universe. When we sit down with Abraham, Isaac and Jacob (see Luke 13:29), there'll be some from the north and the south—borscht and tacos—and from the east and the west—sushi and corn dogs. What language will we speak—or will we all speak all the languages and understand each other perfectly? We're all going to be foreigners in the New Jerusalem. But we're all going to be *home!*

And that's where God is taking us. That's where it's all coming together.

- To summarize: *Some* from every people, tribe, tongue and nation will be in heaven with us. That's a solid fact. John saw in the future that they'll *all* be represented before the throne of the Lamb. And God Himself is registering these representatives—people group by people group.

- How many people groups or *ethne* are yet to have representatives in heaven? That leads us to our second topic: Where we are now in God's great scheme of things.

II. Where We Are Now

What is God doing today to see that some from every people, tribe, tongue and nation celebrate with us in Zion? He's using us to invite everyone to go with us. If we ourselves are glad in the Lord, it's a natural thing to invite other people in our own and other cultures to also be glad—to let them sing for joy.

"Let the peoples praise Thee, O God;

Let all the peoples praise Thee.

Let the nations be glad and sing for joy"

(Psalm 67:3,4).

A. In our day God is calling the peoples of the world to Zion. We don't hear much good news, really, about how God is bringing some from every people—especially in our own culture—to rejoice in Him, to head for the holy city. Maybe that's because the enemy of men's souls doesn't want us to be encouraged.

   - What is God doing today?

(Perhaps have several individuals trade off sharing brief breakthrough after breakthrough. Occasionally refer to a map or globe. The point of this glimpse of what God is doing is not informational but emotional impact; so don't dwell on details or statistics. Choose from among the "Message Breakthroughs" according to your own interests and your time allotment.)

B. The pace of what God is doing is accelerating.

   What's remarkable about our point in history is that the pace of what God is doing seems to be accelerating.

   - (Ask for a show of hands.) How many of us have heard that Islam, the religion of the Muslims, is the fastest growing religion in the world today? The truth is, true Christianity is the fastest growing religion in the world. (Show Overhead 1: Growth of the World's Religious Blocs.)

   - The Body of Christ is spreading like wildfire across the world. Why don't we hear much about it? Because most of that growth isn't in the West. For example: (Show Overhead 2: Growth of Two-Thirds-World Believers.)

   - Even drawing a very general chart of world population tells us something is happening today. (Show Overhead 3: World Population Chart.)

        That abrupt upturn on the chart right at our point

The Sunday Service

in history frightens many with the grim predictions of our global population explosion. But what does it mean from God's perspective?

Of all of His creation, God most highly values the souls of humans. And right now God is suddenly packing into one place at one time more valuable human souls than at any other time in history. And He is allowing those billions of new babies to be born mostly into the Two-Thirds World—which, naturally, is where the Church is now growing like wildfire! What a harvest! (Show Overhead 1: The Growth of True Believers.)

It took more than 1800 years—until 1900—for committed believers in Jesus Christ to become just 2¹/₂ percent of world population. Then it took just 70 years—until 1970—to double and become 5 percent of a much larger world population. Then it took just 22 years—until 1992—to double again and become 10 percent of a much larger world population. More than 400 Christian research centers around the world are monitoring and comparing information right now on just how quickly the Body of Christ is growing.

What is God doing in our world today? He's using believers like us to invite some from every people to a great celebration in a wonderful eternal city, and the pace of those invitations is accelerating: Committed believers are now more than 10 percent of the world population. Let's get a grip on what that means.

A SKIT FOR THE WORLD

What does the real world look like today? You can help clarify the state of the world, encouraging your congregation that committed believers now make up 10 percent of our huge world population, and that for every committed believer today, there are only seven non-Christians worldwide. And you can have some fun at the same time. Here's how. Feel free to ad lib these basic lines and adjust as you desire according to the interactive habits of your congregation.

Say **What does the world look like from God's perspective? We wanted to invite the entire planet's population here, but we'll have to settle for a sample demonstration. First, I need a person with a Bible to stand.**

As a volunteer finally stands, say to her or him **Now open your Bible and look very spiritual. Good.**

Say slowly **Out of every ten people in the world today, one is a committed believer in Jesus Christ. Remember that 10 percent figure? Let's give this person a hand. Now, from this same section I need two more victims—er, volunteers—with Bibles. You two won't have to open your Bibles or look very spiritual.**

Out of every ten people in the world, one is a committed believer..., and two are nominal believers—people who claim Jesus Christ as their personal Lord and Savior and say that they share their faith. But...where's the fruit in their lives? Sure, here they are at a Christian gathering. And they've got Bibles—but do they ever really open them? Papua New Guinea believers call these folks "skin Christians" because it only seems to go skin-deep.

Now, three more volunteers in this same section without Bibles. And you can look as unspiritual as you want.

Summarize **For every one...(point—politely, of course—and pause to let the group name each volunteer) committed believer, there are two...(point and pause) nominal believers. And there are three...pagans! Actually, these are non-Christians within reach of the gospel. They live in cultures where there is a strong Christian witness. Sometimes they live right next door to a committed believer.**

For every ten people in the world, there is one committed believer; two nominal believers; and three non-Christians within reach of the gospel.

(Choose another section of seats or another area of the room to ask for the following volunteers.) Say **Now I need four more volunteers from this section. Good. Now, out of every ten people in the world today, four are serious pagans! Don't they look a little pagan? Seriously, these four are non-Christians beyond the current reach of the gospel. They live in cultures without a strong church or with no church at all. Most of these unreached people groups are Muslim, Hindu, Buddhist, spirit-worshiping tribal groups or minority Chinese groups. Some researchers guess there may be as many as 10,000 people groups who have yet to be invited to the celebrations of heaven. Others say they cluster into about 2,000 least-reached cultural groups.**

And most of them live in what's called "The 10/40 Window"—that area between 10 and 40 degrees north latitudes, from West Africa to the China Sea. (Show Overhead 5: The 10/40 Window.)

(Continued on back)

(Continued from front)

Now, if this is a picture of the world as it is, what needs to happen here? I'll give you 60 seconds to talk with at least two others and come up with an answer to the question "What needs to happen in our world today?" Go!

(Even if your congregation is not used to interacting during a service, allow them to interact at this point. After all, this is a special Sunday. The volunteers remain standing. The ensuing discussion should be stopped short at one minute. Then guide the reporting of ideas toward the following three conclusions.)

Say Among those that name Christ, these nominal believers—these "skin Christians"—need to be challenged to a serious commitment to the Lordship of Christ, right? When those in the church are challenged to repentance and commitment, what's that called? Revival! If there's anything the world needs, it's a revived Church of Jesus Christ. If that's your heart, this is the day for your ministry.

These three non-Christians within reach of the gospel need to clearly and personally be presented the claims of Christ. They live in people groups with churches—such as the English, the Mexican, the Zulu people of South Africa—so they think they have an idea of what Christianity is all about. And it's usually a pretty sad idea. Will they come here to find out the truth? Probably not. Did Jesus ever tell us to sit and wait till they come? What, then, needs to happen? Evangelism—in word and deed! If you have a heart for evangelism, today is your day.

And how about these four serious pagans? These non-Christians who have no clue about a relationship with Jesus Christ? They are the unreached peoples of the world, such as the Sundanese people of Indonesia, the Agul people around the Caspian Sea, or the Deccani people of India. Notice the gap that exists between them and these other six people in cultures that have a gospel witness. Someone needs to cross this gap of culture and present the gospel. And what is that called? Missions!

Thank the participants and lead in polite applause. Say Now let's see the pattern of how God is working—in revival, in evangelism and in missions.

C. God's basic global plan is blessing us to bless every people.

"God be gracious to us and bless us,

And cause His face to shine upon us"

(Psalm 67:1).

- Doesn't that sound familiar? We want God to bless us and that's good. But sometimes we want His blessing so badly we cut off the rest of this sentence. We just want to focus on ourselves.

  Notice your "Thoughts to Ponder" at the top of your Service Notes sheet. What's the rest of "Be still, and..."? Yes, it's "know that I am God." Right? Well, that's the part we like: the "bless-me" part. We want to rest, to be still, knowing He is God, He is in control. But that's not all there is to the rest of the verse. "I will be exalted among the nations; I will be exalted in the earth" (Psalm 46:10, *NIV*).

  The privilege of God's blessing always carries a responsibility, no matter how much we want to ignore it.

  Now back to Psalm 67:1,2. Why should we call out for God to bless us, to be gracious to us and cause His face to shine upon us?

"That Thy way may be known on the earth,

Thy salvation among all nations" (Psalm 67:2).

- Here is that "nations" or "peoples" theme again. Why does God bless us? To bless the nations. Notice:

"God blesses us

That all the ends of the earth may fear Him"

(Psalm 67:7).

- Why does God bless us? So that all the nations, all the people groups invited to eternity with us may come to salvation. Think of all the ways God has blessed you. Those blessings—spiritual, tangible, emotional, experiential—all have a purpose. We are to bless the world's peoples—our own included!

  That breaks down into four categories. Notice on your Service Notes sheet:

  God blesses us, and some of us are to implement that blessing within the church. We need to disciple, encourage, counsel, teach, care for and serve other believers so we'll all be strong. Strong for what?

  The church needs to be strengthened, *revived* to do our job of blessing the nations. One of those nations is our own, our own people, our own culture. Some of us are blessed with gifts and ministries to focus on our

"AND" OR "THAT...?"

The last verse of Psalm 67 in many English translations suggests a very incidental relationship between "God blesses us" and "all the ends of the earth may fear Him" by joining the two clauses with an *and*. But the patterns of Hebrew poetry suggest that the meaning of this last sentence in the poem/psalm circles back to repeat the meaning of the first sentence of verses one and two: "May God be gracious to us and bless us...that Thy way may be known among all nations, Thy salvation among all peoples" (vv. 1,2). Here there is clearly a purpose relationship indicated by *that*.

Probably the *NASB* is closest to the original "purpose" relationship of the clauses in verse seven: "God blesses us, that the ends of the earth may fear Him" (v. 7).

own culture—our city, our country. We're to bless through evangelism, through taking a godly stand on issues, through ministering to the poor, giving a cup of cold water in Jesus' name. We're to be salt and light.

And some of us are blessed to bless the cultures other than our own. They may be overseas; or, since many hundreds of people groups are here in our own country, you might bless those from other people groups right in your own home.

You might feel you can't do much. But you do have a contribution to make—to strengthen the church, to bless our own people, or perhaps to offer the blessing of redemption in Jesus Christ to the other peoples of the world. Your part, added to all the ministry of all of the committed believers worldwide, is very significant. We're inviting the peoples to praise Him. (Emphasize the word "let" in the following verse):

"*Let* the peoples praise Thee…*let* all the peoples

praise Thee

Let the nations be glad and sing for joy"

(**Psalm 67:3,4,** italics added).

As we invite our family members and friends and neighbors and the billions to let them rejoice in Him forever, your part is significant.

In closing, let's look at a familiar verse: Ephesians 2:10.

D. He has blessed me for a specific role in this historic plan.

"For we are God's workmanship, created in Christ

Jesus to do good works, which God prepared in

advance for us to do" (Ephesians 2:10, *NIV*).

There are things which God has prepared in advance for you to do: To strengthen the church, and bring revival here. Or perhaps to impact our own people. Or the peoples of the world. These good works are not just random acts. They're God-designed actions that further the cause of Christ—the plan to see some from every people, tribe, tongue and nation rejoicing before the throne of the Lamb, eating alongside us at the great feast we'll have in our glorious, eternal city.

CLOSING CHALLENGE

(Close as you feel led. You might choose to use one of the following anecdotes or share your own convictions about getting in on God's global plan.)

How do we respond to what God is doing in our world today? We find out more about it. We renew our commitment to pray

for the world. You'll find both options on your Service Notes sheet. As Mary told the servants at the wedding of Cana, "Whatever He says to you, do it" (John 2:5). Mark one or both of those responses, and rejoice: We serve a big God who is very much in control of this world. And He's chosen to let each of us be a part of His great global plan.

(Follow your normal end-of-message protocol at this point. If you share Pastor Selchun's story below and if you often sing a chorus at the close, consider singing together "He Is Lord.")

Optional Closing Anecdotes

Choose from one of the following:

- A young pastor in Zimbabwe has the following tacked on his wall:

I am part of the fellowship of the unashamed. I have Holy Spirit power. The dye has been cast. I have stepped over the line. The decision has been made. I am a disciple of His. I will not look back, let up, slow down, back away or be still.

My past is redeemed, my present makes sense, my future is secure. I am finished and done with low living, sight-walking, small planning, smooth knees, colorless dreams, tamed visions, worldly talking, cheap giving and dwarfed goals.

I no longer need preeminence, prosperity, position, promotion or popularity. I do not have to be right, first, tops, recognized, praised, regarded or rewarded. I now live by faith, lean on His presence, walk by patience, am uplifted by prayer and labor by power.

My face is set, my gait is fast, my goal is heaven. My road is narrow, my way rough, my Guide reliable, my mission clear. I cannot be bought, compromised, detoured, lured away, turned back, deluded or delayed. I will not give up, shut up or let up. I will go on until He comes, and work until He stops me.

I am a disciple of Jesus.

Bob Morehead, "Commitment as a Christian," a tract from Hands for Christ, Roanoke, Virginia.

- In northeastern Nigeria, a rash of persecution in August 1993 saw 100 churches burned, some with believers inside. Hundreds were killed and more than 60,000 Christians were left homeless, run out of their villages and towns. In one village young Pastor Selchun was found by Hausa Muslim warriors as he carried his Bible in his right hand. They dragged him to the middle of the village and called all the people out. They forced his wife and sister to watch as they set out a tree stump and pushed the pastor down in front of it. They placed his right hand on the wood block and a warrior raised his sword, shouting, "This is what comes to you Christians for carrying your Bibles!" And with that, he swung the sword and chopped off Pastor Selchun's hand.

FYI: NIGERIA BACKGROUND

In mid-1995 eight churches were burned to the ground in Yobe State in northeastern Nigeria. A pastor and several believers were killed, Christians' cars and motorcycles were destroyed, and the houses of Christians were looted by Muslim mobs.

The vast majority of Muslims are not fanatics, but in this area there are mobs of mostly Hausa fanatics intent on Nigeria becoming an Islamic country. In 1960 Nigeria was 50 percent Muslim, 10 percent Christian and the rest spirit-worshipers. Today Nigeria is still 50 percent Muslim. But it is also 50 percent Christian—which is why the political struggles ensue.

Throughout the 1995 crisis the Christians did not retaliate, and many moderate Muslims have expressed horror at the outrages.

The Sunday Service

Bystanders say that without blinking an eye, Pastor Selchun raised his left hand and began to sing: "He is Lord, He is Lord. He is risen from the dead and He is Lord. Every knee shall bow, every tongue confess..."

- Hundreds of years ago, the great French missionary Francis Xavier was dying. After establishing communities of believers in India (that are thriving to this day) and founding Christian education in Japan, this man of God had come to China. But as he awaited permission to begin ministry, he fell ill. A friend whispered to the great old man dying thousands of miles from home, "Francis, oh, that you could return home to Paris."

Xavier whispered back, "Oh, Paris. If I could but be in Paris again. I would walk the streets of the city through the day and into the night, and in the darkness I would swing my lantern and call out to the students on every street, 'Give up...your small...ambitions!'"

For the sake of the Name, give up small ambitions. For the night is coming when none of us will work anymore.

MESSAGE BREAKTHROUGHS

Choose a few of the most appropriate for your fellowship:

- The number of people who are being presented the plan of salvation every day is now at least 260,274. Pray for today's quarter million plus. May they respond to the call of Christ.

- Over 700 million people in 220 countries have seen the *Jesus* film, with 41,000,000 indicating a commitment to Jesus Christ and to follow-up Bible studies.

- Asia is awakening to the truth in Jesus Christ. Although the numbers of Bibles distributed worldwide sank more than three percent in 1994, the number distributed in Asian and Pacific countries increased by more than 21 percent.

- In recent years, the best-selling book in Japan is the Bible. In a government survey, Japanese citizens were asked to name the greatest religious leader in history. Sixty-seven percent replied, "Jesus Christ."

- In May 1995, 80,000 Korean young people gathered in the Olympic Stadium in Seoul to publicly commit themselves to give at least two years to world evangelization. Another 25,000 later signed the same commitment to make the total 105,000.

- Mongolia, which had no church at all as recently as 1991, now has more than 3,000 believers in 17 congregations. And the Mongolians have sent their first two missionaries to work with Operation Mobilization in India.

- In China's Ningxia (*ning*-sha) Province, the persecution of the Cultural Revolution left only 10 believers meeting regularly in 1979. In April 1985, two elders and five deacons were serving in six reopened churches in the province. There were about a thousand Christians without a single pastor in the province. In May 1990, there were 10,000 Protestant believers. An estimate made recently by the evangelical magazine *Bridge* is 50,000 believers in Ningxia—200 percent growth in less than a decade.

- Within the past five years the Hmong of Vietnam were listed as a people unreached by the gospel. Today more than 330,000 of the total Hmong population of 500,000 have been brought to faith in Christ. Pray for these fellow believers as they are being imprisoned, beaten and ordered to no longer listen to Christian radio broadcasts such as those on Far East Broadcasting Corporation. Pray also for the continued strengthening of the many Hmong churches among refugees in North America.

- In Laos in 1994, with relaxed restrictions from the Marxist government, believers personally presented the gospel to more than 45,000 lowland Lao, and 3,000 committed their lives to Christ. Twenty new churches were established, 1,000 of the new converts were baptized, and 400 were formally trained in evangelism and church-planting. Alarmed at this growth, the government in 1995 clamped down again, jailing believers and closing down churches.

- In Cambodia, ravaged by the communists' 1975-85 execution of more than two million—half the population—the Khmer Church is finding revival. Teams of Khmer believers from the U.S. have found overwhelming openness to the gospel. In a recent baptismal service, 137 new believers were baptized, representing the cooperating ministries of such diverse groups as the Christian Missionary Alliance, Youth With A Mission, Methodists and the *Jesus* film project.

- In Nagaland in India, it is estimated 95 percent of the state's three million people confess Jesus as Lord. The Naga Church has vowed to send out 10,000 new missionaries to the rest of India and to the world.

- The Gospel Association for India, a coalition of Indian ministries, held its forty-ninth annual evangelism crusade in Vijayawada. About 50,000 attended the final night of meetings under a tent the size of three football fields, and 25,000 were brought to faith in Christ during the week. Follow-up crusades are being held in 150 towns and villages.

- In Nepal, a Hindu priest who was miraculously brought to faith in Christ has written a powerful tract comparing Christianity and Hinduism. Thousands of Nepali of various people groups are being brought to Christ as a result. A recent open-air evangelistic crusade in Kathmandu was attended by more than 40,000. In this country where just a few years ago such activity would have meant prison, nearly 2,000 made commitments to Jesus Christ in that one meeting.

- In Central Asia, a church planted in Uzbekistan just four years ago has grown to 3,000 members and has planted 55 other congregations.

- In the former Soviet Union, Christian Broadcasting Network (CBN) has been laboring in a tremendous harvest: Through television ministries in the past few years, more than 30 million in the Commonwealth of Independent States have been brought from darkness into His great light. Often the CBN mail processing center receives 50,000 letters in a single day requesting follow-up materials such as Bible correspondence courses. Pray for the nurturing of this great harvest.

- *USA Today* reports: "In Russia, religious resurgence is so strong that Russia's 65,000 principals, teachers and administrators are now required by the government to attend a course on Bible-based ethics. Officials say up to 55 percent of Russian teachers, many of whom were former atheists, have made personal commitments to Christ. Many are using the New Testament in schools. Natasha Popova tells her 27 students at public school number 42, 'Jesus Christ is God's Son, and He died for our sins. He is alive today and can be your best friend.'"

- Believers are learning to pray for God's protection in the worst of circumstances. In 1995 in Grozny, capital of the rebel Chechnya region of Russia, a dedicated pastor's son was picking his way through the demolished streets of the city. Suddenly he heard a whine, then the sound like thunder of an approaching Russian fighter-bomber. The craft whizzed overhead and fired a missile at the ground. The rocket blasted directly toward him. He leaped a few feet and fell to the ground, covering his head. The missile smashed into the street, burrowing into the ground only a few meters from the young man, spraying dirt all over him. It did not explode.

- A recent report from the Arab world urges believers worldwide to get ready for new breakthrough opportunities to reach Muslims for Christ. Arab Christian leader Abu Wasiim says, "The Spirit of God is moving in currents across the Arab world." Veteran worker Cancy Murphy, says, "We are in the generation in which the Arab world will dramatically see a spiritual breakthrough." Luis Bush of the A.D. 2000 and Beyond movement, says "It is time for God's people around the world to get ready. Undoubtedly a spiritual breakthrough in the Arab world is coming."

- Pray for believers in Saudi Arabia, probably the most restrictive country in the world when it comes to Christianity. Rumors of pilgrims to Mecca having dreams and visions of Jesus Christ were made more plausible by the testimony of an Indonesian who "heard Jesus speak to him" while in Mecca. The man is now back in Indonesia, has come to faith in Christ and was recently baptized.

- Pray for the 12 million Middle Eastern believers persecuted and imprisoned in several countries hostile to the gospel. In a letter out of a Middle Eastern prison, a believer imprisoned for the past eight years writes:

   "I thank my loving God that He counted me worthy to keep me here because of my faith in the Lord Jesus Christ, and I thank my brothers and sisters who have supported me in prayer that victory may bring glory to the Lord. During Christmas one of the guards asked, 'Does Jesus know He has a lover here, too?' I told him that Jesus has millions of lovers all over the world who are willing to sacrifice their lives for Him.

"I tell you...it is a sort of waste to leave this world by natural death. What a privilege to live for our Lord and to sacrifice our lives for Him. I am prepared, for the name of Jesus Christ, not only to remain in prison but also to give my life in His service."

What a challenge to our commitment.

- In Bordeaux, France in the summer of 1993, 1700 believers from 33 countries committed themselves through "The Bordeaux Declaration" to reach for Christ the 500 million French-speaking people in 50 countries through church planting and evangelization. At a 1995 follow-up conference in Cote d'Ivoire (the Ivory Coast), 2,000 Christian leaders planning details of this massive evangelistic outreach were moved as two Christian Hutu and Tutsi leaders embraced each other in reconciliation after the horrors of Rwanda's civil war.

- Is God working among every nation—even in strictly Islamic Libya? An Iraqi Christian reports that four Libyan Arab believers who work in the oil fields began meeting about a year and a half ago for prayer before work. They meet six days a week beside a loud diesel tractor, so the noise of the engine covers the sound of their prayer time. Within 14 months, the number of believers among the oil workers grew to 16. Now there are about 60 new believers meeting for prayer beside the tractor. The Italian oil field supervisor found out about the group and arranged for a Malta pastor to be flown in once a month to minister to this new oil patch church in the heartland of Libya.

- In Ethiopia, 11 denominations have joined to make sure each of the 80 unreached peoples of this country have a solid gospel witness. Unified prayer times at 5 A.M. each morning and whole-church bi-weekly prayer sessions are breaking through cultural barriers. In one area a large tree was the central focus of the people's spirit worship. The children were trained to kiss the tree and say, "This tree saved me." When local believers began uniting in prayer against the tree worship, in spite of an extensive root system and location beside a river, the tree dried up and fell into the river. Locals were shocked and exclaimed, "Your God made this tree uproot and dry up." And as a result about a hundred in that community have been brought to faith in Jesus Christ.

- What "crowns of rejoicing" will you enjoy in our great city of Zion? The legacy of now-retired missionaries Doug and Evelyn Knapp is nothing short of amazing: The Knapps' ministry in Tanzania over the past decades resulted in 58,144 new believers being baptized. And these believers believe in discipling others: Recently a 15-day evangelism emphasis by these resulted in another 4,100 coming to faith in Jesus Christ. And this was in a country where the current head of state is Muslim, where the media avidly promote Islam, and Christian open-air meetings have been banned.

- Nineteen sixty-three wasn't all that long ago. At that time, Nigeria was 50 percent Muslim, 10 percent Christian and the rest spirit-worshiping. Today Nigeria is still 50 percent Muslim. But it is now also 50 percent Christian. Pray for the current religious and political see-saw in this most populous nation of Africa.

- In Algeria the Berbers, a mega-people group usually thought to be very resistant to the gospel, now has thousands of believers in Jesus Christ. Factual accounts of the spiritual awakening tell of churches spreading like wildfire particularly in the Atlas Mountains, and of marathon outdoor prayer sessions attended by several thousand new believers.

- Puerto Rico now has the highest number of evangelicals per square mile of any country in the world. Of the country's 3.5 million people, one million are evangelicals. They have 7,000 churches, 10,000 pastors, nine Christian TV stations, 13 Christian radio stations, 130 Christian schools and 350 Christian community service organizations. More than 1,000

Puerto Rican young people called Las Catacumbas are now training to go as missionaries to Muslims.

- In Buenos Aires, Argentina, the church "Ondas de Amor y Paz" (Waves of Love and Peace) attracts 225,000 people each week. Services take place daily in a converted movie theater from 9 A.M. to midnight, and every month another 3,000 new believers are baptized.

- One hundred years ago, there were no evangelical churches in Brazil. In 1980 there were about 12 million Protestants. By 1995, that number had increased to more than 40 million, with more than 80,000 churches and 150 Christian radio and TV stations. The number is expected to reach 50 million by the year 2000. At least five new evangelical churches open every week now in Rio de Janeiro. At the same time, the Brazilian evangelical mission force has mushroomed, from 1,000 to more than 2,500 missionaries in the past five years alone.

- Finally enjoying a period of peace, El Salvadorans are streaming out to evangelistic events. Recently, in the largest gathering in the history of El Salvador, 130,000 crammed into a soccer stadium designed to hold 80,000 to hear a local pastor proclaim the gospel. Thousands came to faith in Christ, and the continuing revival prompted Christian workers to exult that "almost 30 percent of the population is born again *so far.*"

- What's happening in North America? In spite of the doom and gloom even the Christian media tend to foist on American Christians:

—Eighty-five million copies of the *New International Version* of the Bible have been sold in the past 15 years; and 42 percent of its purchasers read the Bible every day.

—Every week 34 percent of the American population reads the Bible outside of church—that's 75 million weekly exposed to the Word that "will not return void".

From a *Times-Mirror* survey: Of the American adults surveyed (3,517):

—Eighty-three percent agreed that "we will all be called before God at the judgment day to answer for our sins."

—Seventy-six percent agreed that "There are guidelines about what's good and evil that apply to everyone regardless of their situation."

On an average day Americans buy 35,932 Bibles.

The Annual Barna Report states that "Fifty-six percent [of Americans] believe the Bible is the written word of God and is totally accurate in what it says."

But for the first time in 50 years the number of American career missionaries has dropped—from 50,500 in 1988 to 41,142 in 1992. Veteran missionaries who went out after World War II are retiring now in droves, and they're not being replaced—yet.

OVERHEAD #1

GROWTH RATE
OF THE WORLD'S RELIGIOUS BLOCS

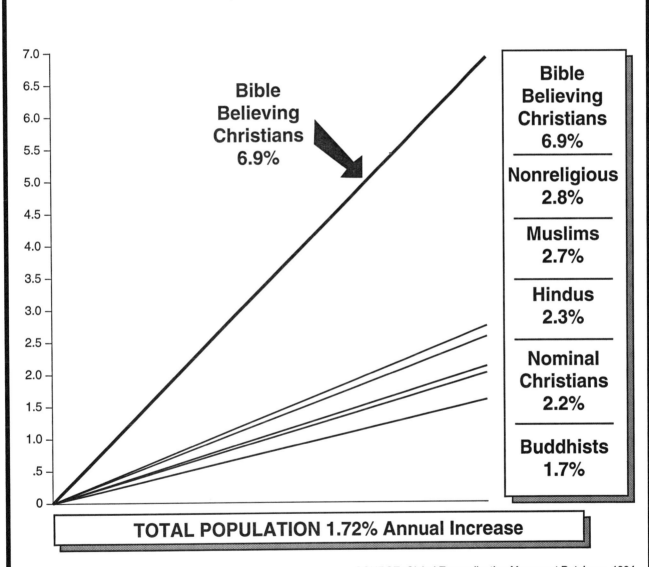

Bible Believing Christians 6.9%

Bible Believing Christians	**6.9%**
Nonreligious	**2.8%**
Muslims	**2.7%**
Hindus	**2.3%**
Nominal Christians	**2.2%**
Buddhists	**1.7%**

TOTAL POPULATION 1.72% Annual Increase

SOURCE: Global Evangelization Movement Database, 1994

OVERHEAD #2

GROWTH OF TWO-THIRDS-WORLD BELIEVERS

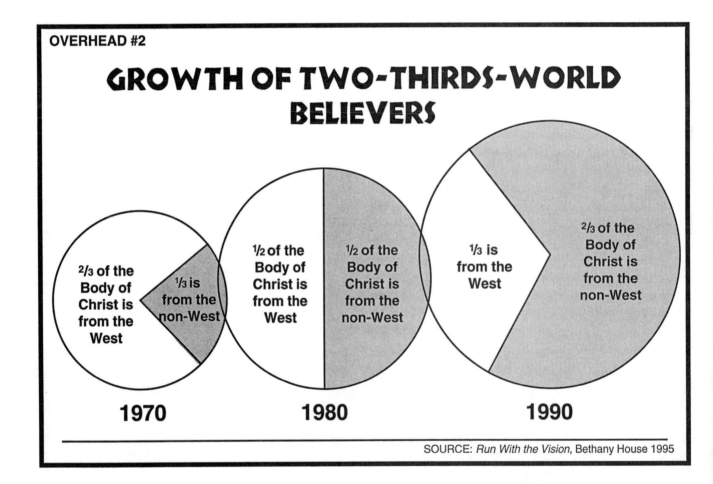

2/3 of the Body of Christ is from the West

1/3 is from the non-West

1970

1/2 of the Body of Christ is from the West

1/2 of the Body of Christ is from the non-West

1980

1/3 is from the West

2/3 of the Body of Christ is from the non-West

1990

SOURCE: *Run With the Vision*, Bethany House 1995

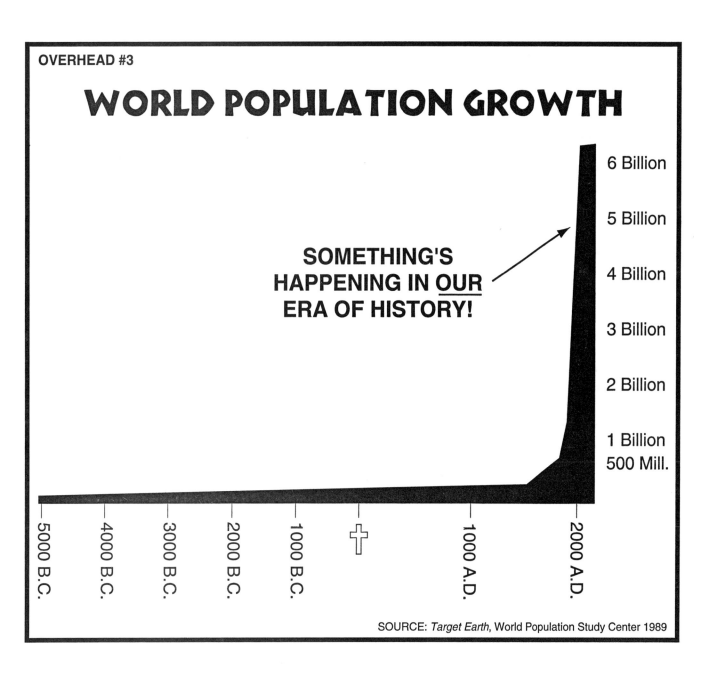

WORLD POPULATION GROWTH

OVERHEAD #3

SOMETHING'S HAPPENING IN OUR ERA OF HISTORY!

6 Billion
5 Billion
4 Billion
3 Billion
2 Billion
1 Billion
500 Mill.

5000 B.C.   4000 B.C.   3000 B.C.   2000 B.C.   1000 B.C.   ✝   1000 A.D.   2000 A.D.

SOURCE: *Target Earth*, World Population Study Center 1989

OVERHEAD #4

GROWTH OF TRUE BELIEVERS

2½%

5%

10%

A.D. 50-1900
It took 1850 years for true believers to become 2½% of world population.

1900-1970
Then it took just 70 years for that percentage to double to 5% of a much larger world population.

1970-1992
Then it took just 22 years to double again to become 10% of a much larger world population!

SOURCE: *Mission Frontiers*, U.S. Center for World Mission, 1993

OVERHEAD #5

THE 10/40 WINDOW

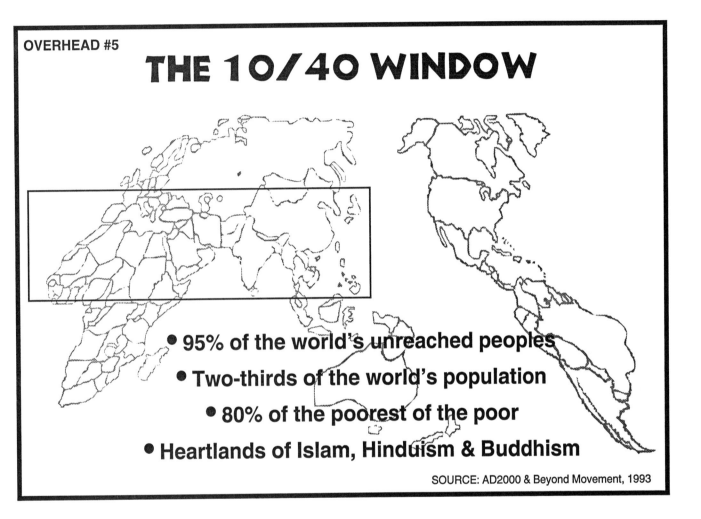

- 95% of the world's unreached peoples
- Two-thirds of the world's population
- 80% of the poorest of the poor
- Heartlands of Islam, Hinduism & Buddhism

SOURCE: AD2000 & Beyond Movement, 1993

HEAVEN IS A
WONDERFUL PLACE

WELCOME TO *A SUNDAY FOR THE WORLD*

Some "Hmmmm...?" thoughts to ponder before the service:

- In heaven, will we still look like we're from various ethnic groups?
- Finish this familiar verse: "Be still, and...." Look up Psalm 46:10, *NIV*, to see if you're correct.

God is in control. He knows what He's doing with us and He knows where He's leading us. And that's what today's *A Sunday for the World* celebration is all about:

1. Where we are going;
2. Where we are now in God's great scheme of things.

WHERE WE ARE GOING
(REVELATION 21 – 22:2)

- Heaven is real and a wonderful place.
- The heavenly city's inhabitants are from every people group (see Revelation 5:9).
- God keeps a registration list of those heading for the city (see Psalm 87:2-6).

WHERE WE ARE NOW

- In our day God is calling the peoples of the world to live in His city.
- The pace of what God is doing is accelerating.
- He's doing it by blessing us to bless every people (see Psalm 67:1,2,7).
- He has blessed me for a specific role in this historic plan (see Ephesians 2:10, *NIV*).

So?

How do we get in on what God is doing in the big picture? Here are some strategic options:

_____ I'd like to get into a group Bible study on this topic.

_____ This week I will help pass on God's blessing to the nations by taking a Prayer Guide to someone who couldn't be here today.

_____ This week I will get my family (or I will put together a "family") to learn more from the Family Activity Guide.

167

PRAY FOR THE TURKMEN

During *A Sunday for the World*, we found that there are 2,000 clusters of perhaps 10,000 people groups without the gospel. (If you were unable to attend *A Sunday for the World* and your church tape records its services, be sure to ask for a tape of the *A Sunday for the World* message.) These are the remaining "nations" Jesus talked about in Matthew 28:19,20:

> "Go therefore and make disciples of all the
> nations [in the original Greek, *ethne*] baptizing
> them in the name of the Father, and the Son and
> the Holy Spirit, teaching them to observe all that
> I commanded you."

And we reminded ourselves that one of the most powerful things we can do to see believers from every people, tribe, tongue and nation in heaven (see Revelation 5:9) is to pray more specifically.

This week will you please pray for the Turkmen, one of the world's unreached people groups? Perhaps you have significant amounts of time to devote to this important strategy of prayer—time others of us don't seem to have.

We'll be counting on you to uphold this very necessary ministry of our congregation—global prayer.

THE TURKMEN:
A HARD, FRIGHTENED PEOPLE

This Central Asian desert people say about themselves, "Look at the heart of a horse. It is big and tough. No wonder the horse is a fearless animal—feeling no emotion. Then look at the heart of a man. It is small and soft. No wonder he is easily frightened and hurt. Only a few people have really hard hearts. The heart in a chicken is very small like a man's, and so it is easily frightened." And to strengthen their "easily frightened" hearts, the men of this people devour raw chicken hearts to toughen themselves, to strengthen and enlarge their own hearts.

Only a hundred years ago, Europeans held that the Turkmen were "more like wild beasts than men, who have no sense of fear and will never submit; even their women and children will die fighting."

Since the 10th century, the Turkmen have been frequently invaded by Mongols, Persians and other peoples; they have developed strong military skills and a mostly nomadic lifestyle. They became the dread of Central Asia, with a reputation as marauding brigands who preyed upon caravans and indulged in slave trading. The Turkmen have been so isolated in their arid desert that some who were displaced by the

Prayer Guide

THE TURKMEN: AN UNREACHED PEOPLE

- They have not heard. Turkmenistan's few Russian and Armenian Christians have not reached out to the ethnic Turkmen. Some Turkmen in refugee camps in Pakistan have been ministered to by Christian relief groups.
- There is some Scripture available—a John's Gospel and a New Testament published in 1993.
- They have no church. Among the total 4 million Turkmen, there are perhaps 30 to 40 Christians in a few scattered families.

FOR FURTHER STUDY

- "Horsemen of the Steppes." *National Geographic*, Nov. 1973.
- Soviet Peoples map supplement. *National Geographic*, Feb. 1976.
- "Turkmen Nomads." *Natural History*, 77:9, 1968.
- Weekes, Richard. *Muslim Peoples*. London: Greenwood Press, 1978.
- Barthold, V.V. *A History of the Turkmen People*. Leiden: E.J. Brill, 1962.

1980s fighting in Afghanistan were shocked to find theirs was not the only language in the world.

Although the USSR in 1924 claimed them as Soviet citizens, Turkmen were always a problem to count, tax or conscript into the Soviet army. Since the breakup of the Soviet Union in 1991, Turkmenistan has been a fiercely independent country. The exodus of hundreds of Russian professionals has jeopardized the already at-risk medical, economic and civil structures of the country. Yet often their pride keeps them from asking for help.

About 1.4 million Turkmen live in other countries such as Iran—where they are known as "Turkomen"—and even in England and the U.S. In Turkmenistan itself, about half of the 2.5 million Turkmen live around the Black Sand Desert. They herd sheep and goats, grow cotton and make some of the finest carpets in Central Asia. The other half are city dwellers who largely have been Russified, living in Soviet-style, gray block buildings and working at various trades—oil and gas, retail merchandising, civil service, etc.—as in any formerly Russian-dominated city in Central Asia.

Since the breakup of the Soviet Union, the Turkmen's serious economic situation has worsened. And yet they sit atop tremendous oil and gas reserves.

Turkmen all claim to be Sunni Muslims. But Islam is only a thin veneer over occult practices involving mediums, magic, charms and curses. Fear of the "evil eye" and of evil spirits inspires them to undergo magic rituals to protect themselves and their families. The secular, communist-style government officially allows freedom of religion, yet is suspicious of any Christian influence.

Turkmen are a hard, proud people who have never been loved. They have virtually never been approached as a people with the love of Christ.

The tough yet inwardly "easily frightened" Turkmen are without God and without hope.

PRAY FOR TURKMEN
Matthew 9:37,38

- Pray that God will break the bondages of fear, inferiority and aggression that keep this people isolated—except from the increasing influence of Islamic forces from Iran. Pray they'll find their true strength in Christ.
- Pray for the release of the Turkmen from superstition and the occult—spiritual forces beneath the religious facade of Islam. Pray for the tearing down of the "shroud" of darkness (see Isaiah 25:7, *NIV*) over this people that has kept their minds blinded (see 2 Corinthians 4:4). Fear, ritual and superstition hold Turkmen captive to empty answers and teach that God is impersonal and unknowable. Pray that God will reveal Himself in power, exposing the powerlessness of Islam for salvation and confirming the absolute truth of the gospel of Jesus Christ.

- Old age is highly respected among the Turkmen. Pray that God will reveal Himself to the elders, the religious leaders and heads of households so that entire families will turn to Christ. Pray that older believers from the West will go to minister in Turkmenistan.

- Pray for believers who will go and demonstrate to the Turkmen the reality, presence and character of God in Jesus Christ. Pray for God to send forth Christian teachers and students, oil and gas workers, economic and legal consultants, agriculturists, health and medical personnel, artists and musicians, water specialists and tourists. Then pray for a wave of evangelists and church-planters.

- Pray for laborers and the permission they need to distribute the Turkmen New Testament, Gospel of John and the *Jesus* film and video.

- Pray for those now preparing Turkmen gospel radio programs.

- Pray for true believers—local Russians or Armenians or other foreigners in Turkmenistan or in other countries—to reach out to the Turkmen in the name of Christ.

Full-color prayer cards depicting the Turkmen and other unreached peoples are available from William Carey Library, call 800-MISSION. For more information about reaching the Turkmen for Christ, contact: Caleb Project, 10 W. Dry Creek Circle, Littleton, CO 80120-4413; Phone: 303-730-4170 Fax: 303-730-4177, Internet: Info@cproject.com.

THE LAND OF TURKMENISTAN

- Area: 488,100 sq. km.—the size of Great Britain
- Capital: Ashkabad
- Nine tenths of the land is the Kara Kum (Black Sand) Desert, with oases along the rivers and canal banks.
- Less than 1/10 of the land is suitable for growing cotton and grazing sheep.
- Region has reserves of oil and natural gas.

THE TURKMEN PEOPLE

- Population—Total four million
- 2.5 million in Turkmenistan
- Approximate numbers outside Turkmenia:
  - —100,000 in Uzbekistan
  - —400,000 in Afghanistan
  - —50,000 from Afghanistan in Pakistani refugee camps
  - —500,000 in Iran
  - —500,000 in Iraq
  - —300,000 in Turkey
  - —82,000 in Tibet
  - —1,000 in Germany
  - —2,000 in the U.S.

IN TURKMENISTAN

- Forty-five percent urban, rest rural
- Average household 4.2 persons, 480,000 households
- Fifty-one percent have some secondary education
- Religion: 99.5 percent Sunni-Hanafi Muslim, prevalent paganism and shamanism

FROM INDIA TO CAIRO

Go ahead. Commit yourself to two eight-minute family sessions to reinforce your children's and your own insights into God's heart for the unreached peoples of the earth. The guide is designed in a one-size-fits-all format for families with any age children. If you don't have children, borrow some!

In each session you'll need a Bible, paper and pencils. If possible have a globe or world map to refer to.

During the sessions or at any time, encourage your family members to learn the "Psalm 67 Song" to reinforce the lessons of *A Sunday for the World*.

PSALM 67 SONG

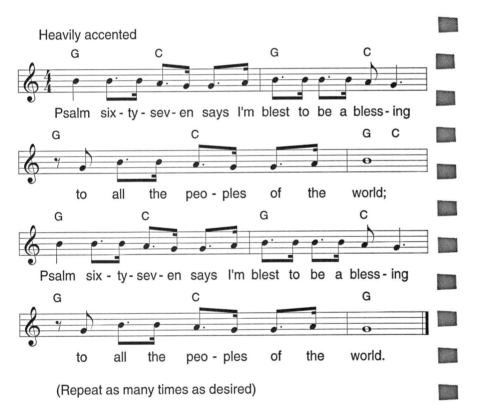

Heavily accented

Psalm six - ty - sev - en says I'm blest to be a bless - ing to all the peo - ples of the world;

Psalm six - ty - sev - en says I'm blest to be a bless - ing to all the peo - ples of the world.

(Repeat as many times as desired)

FAMILY ACTIVITY SESSION 1

Today's story is geared to a young age level; so older youth have a Thought Project to chew on. Read the story or have an older child read. With toddlers, simply emphasize in your own simple words the basic story line as outlined in bold print.

THE STORY

In southern India, **11-year-old Subhas** Reddi **stands nervously in the front room of his home** while the Hindu priest chants a mantra, a few words repeated over and over. **Subhas thinks there are hundreds of gods, and he wants all of them to bless him** as he goes through one of the most important ceremonies of his life. **A little seven-year-old girl stands next to him. She's dressed in a beautiful, green sari, a dress made by wrapping 15 to 18 feet of cloth around and around her.**

After the chanting, **Subhas places a gold bracelet around her wrist. All the parents at the ceremony smile and lead the two children to a great feast—a wedding feast, because Subhas and the little girl are now married!**

Living in the state of Andhra Pradesh in India, **Subhas and his new bride are from the wealthy Pakanati Reddis,** an unreached people group with a population of 25,000. Unlike most Indians, the Pakanati Reddis have color televisions, refrigerators and vast farmlands. The group encourages child marriages even though it is against Indian law. This way wealthy parents can arrange to keep their money, houses and land in the tribe. **Little girls are often married to cousins or uncles to keep the money in the family.** In some cases, parents even kidnap boys from wealthier families and marry them to their infant daughters.

In the past few years, some other tribes of the Reddis have received Christ, but so far **no one from the Pakanati Reddis has become a Christian.**

THE ACTIVITY

If you have a world map, find the state of Andhra Pradesh in southern India. Preschoolers have no concept of "the other side of the world" much less how a flat poster on a wall is the ground they walk on, so think of this map exercise as a long-range training activity.

As in a "Pictionary" game, draw your idea of "a wedding ceremony" or "wedding" while the others try to guess what you're drawing. If they haven't guessed in 30 seconds, tell the answer. Choose another artist, whisper instructions that he or she is to draw "love of money" or just "money" and allow another 30 seconds for guesses. Then simply read:

Among the Pakanati Reddis, belief in Hindu gods and the love of money are strong barriers to the gospel.

THE BIBLE PASSAGE

Read 1 Timothy 6:7-11.

PRAYER

Lead in prayer as you join hands; kneel together and encourage all to pray aloud or pray silently with the youngest saying "Amen" when you pat him or her.

- Pray for Subhas and his bride to hear about Christ.
- Pray for efforts by Christians in related Reddi tribes to reach the Pakanati Reddis.
- Pray that we won't worship things or money as "gods."

TEENAGERS' THOUGHT PROJECT

Reaching every people group in the world seems impossible. But if you kept your ears open during the *A Sunday for the World* activities, you know that seemingly impossible problems can sometimes be solved very simply. We can reach every people for Christ, just as you can solve this problem:

The Old Story

Bimal, traveling through India with a sack of grain, a goat and a wolf, must cross a river in a canoe that can only carry him and one other item at a time. Without any outside solutions such as getting help or tying up an animal, how can Bimal take all three across one at a time without the wolf eating the goat or the goat eating the grain? (It can be done. If you can't figure it out, see if your minister can solve the riddle for you.)

India Focus: India has 1,658 languages and the most unreached people groups of any region in the world.

Look what God is doing: Think of a city with a population of 15,000. Every month that many new believers are baptized in India—but so far none among the Pakanati Reddis.

Family Activity

OPTIONAL ACTIVITIES

- Encourage the females in your family to try wrapping themselves in a sheet to make their own version of a sari.
- Add a touch of curry powder—a common flavoring in Indian dishes—to a casserole you're cooking.
- Check out from your local library well-illustrated periodicals such as *National Geographic* that have articles on India and leave these on tables around the house.

PRAYER

Pray for the Pakanati Reddis of India, one of the world's remaining unreached peoples. Some of them will come to Christ (see Revelation 5:9), so we know it's God's will to reach them and we can pray confidently (see 1 John 5:14,15).

FAMILY ACTIVITY SESSION 2

Read the story or have an older child read. With toddlers, simply emphasize in your own words the basic story line outlined in bold print.

THE STORY

What country was it where Pharaoh's daughter found the baby Moses in a little boat in the bullrushes?

Egypt is the country, and its captial is Cairo. It's a dusty city, with streets lined with palm trees that look like old upside-down dust mops. The winding alleyways of the market bazaars and the suburb streets seem always clogged in traffic jams of little battered compact cars from Europe. Exhaust fumes billow through the 90-degree morning heat of the *khamsin* (kom'-sin), the hot sandy wind blowing in from the surrounding desert.

Bright sunlight flickers on the huge, green river in the middle of the city; it shines on the white triangle-shaped lateen sails of the barges. **What's the name of the river? It's the old, old Nile—where Moses was hidden 3,000 years ago.**

People hurry to work on the streets this morning; they seem tired. Men in slightly threadbare suits hang from old streetcars, going to office jobs and stores in the city of nearly 12 million—just as millions of people do in every big city in the world.

Down a side street, little dark-eyed, black-haired Amina hurries to her Islamic fundamentalist **school.** Islam—meaning "yielded to Allah"—is a religion that teaches Jesus—*Isa* (ee-sa) (their name for Him)—isn't God, and wasn't as important as Allah's prophet Mohammed. Ten-year-old Amina is a Muslim, someone who follows Islam. She's excited because today her teacher has chosen her to lead the class in what American children might call a "pledge of allegiance."

Arriving at school, Amina shakes the khamsin sand from her clothes, **steps to a microphone and says, "We will answer the call of Islam, and all be sacrificed for Islam."** The other children then say, **"We will change society and the evil in it."**

Family Activity

Amina, her classmates and teachers all have been taught that some of the evil in their society comes from Christians. Christians are their holy enemies. After all, it was the Christians during the Holy Crusades that slaughtered thousands of Turkish Muslims in order to recapture Jerusalem. These modern fundamentalist Muslim Brotherhood sects have violently persecuted Christians ever since Egypt's president Sadat declared peace with Israel in 1979. Even Sadat was killed as an enemy of strict Islam.

Muslims are taught that Christians believe in a trinity of three Gods: the Father, the Son, and the Mother Mary. No wonder Christianity is suspect.

In Egypt and most other Islamic countries, Christians can legally worship but can't legally talk to others about Christianity. Still, each year hundreds of Muslims in Cairo, especially university students, turn to Christ.

Poor Amina. She thinks we Christians hate her! Let's pray that Amina and other Muslim children will meet Christians who will show her the love of Jesus.

THE ACTIVITY

- Find Cairo on your map.
- Pick someone to be Amina and for just a minute or two role-play a scene:

    Amina says, "I hate you Christians because you hate us Muslims. And you don't worship the one true God."

    How do the rest of your family members answer? Act it out; then on your own study books on ministry to Muslims to find out how you might more effectively answer.

THE BIBLE PASSAGE

Read Isaiah 19:19-22.

PRAYER

Lead in prayer as you join hands; kneel together and encourage all to pray aloud or pray silently with the youngest saying "Amen" when you pat him or her.

- Pray that the children and leaders of the strict Muslims living in Cairo will be willing to listen to the true claims of Christ.
- Pray that some of the 8 million Christians in Egypt will be able to convince Amina and her family that Christians are not their enemies and that Isa—Jesus Christ—is the way, the truth and the life.
- Pray that the Christians in Egypt and other Islamic countries will respond in courage and love when they are persecuted for Christ's sake.

TEENAGERS' THOUGHT PROJECT

Let's say Christians get radical and obedient and make disciples out of every unreached people group—which is what we were told to do in Matthew 28:19. How tough a job is it? Compute the following figures:

- At the time of the Acts 2 Day of Pentecost, there was one church—which was commanded to reach what we guess was about 60,000 unreached people groups with the gospel! How many people groups would that church have to reach to finish the job?

Churches   Unreached People Groups

The Ratio: _____ for every _____

- Today, there are about 7 million churches of committed believers worldwide and 2,000 clusters of unreached people groups left. What's the ratio of churches to people groups now? (Divide 2,000 by 7,000,000.)

Churches   Unreached People Groups

The Ratio: _____ for every _____

Does the job seem possible? What could happen if those churches got their heads together? Will you do anything about this big-picture project to bless every people? Why or why not?

Egypt Focus

Egypt has a 17 percent Christian population that is declining because many believers are leaving the country for North America, Europe and Australia. About 150 missionaries work in Egypt in 27 agencies, and evangelical congregations within Egypt support about 25 missionaries.

Look What God Is Doing

During a recent summertime evangelistic effort, more than 25,000 Muslims in rural areas of Egypt came to faith in Jesus Christ. Pray for these new believers as they face stiff persecution, and pray for similar breakthroughs among militant Muslims in Cairo.

OPTIONAL ACTIVITIES

- Get instructions and basket-making materials at a craft supply store and weave baby-Moses-bullrushes cradles for family members' dolls.
- Practice greeting each other in Arabic with: "Salaam a leikum!" (sah-lam uh-lay-ee-koom) which means "Peace be upon you." The response is: "Wa aleikum salaam" (wah uh-lay-ee-koom sah-lam), which means, "And unto you be peace."
- Check out from your local library well-illustrated periodicals such as *National Geographic* or *Aramco World* that have articles on Egypt and the Arab world.

PRAYER

Pray for the Egyptian Muslims of Cairo. Some of them will come to Christ (see Revelation 5:9), so we know it's God's will to reach them and we can pray confidently (see 1 John 5:14,15).

IT CAN BE DONE: BASIC PRINCIPLES IN GOD'S GLOBAL PLAN

KEY VERSE

"The promise is for you and your children, and for all who are far off, as many as the Lord our God shall call to Himself." Acts 2:39

KEY BIBLE PASSAGES

Genesis 12:1-3; Psalm 67:1,2,7; Isaiah 61:1; Matthew 28:18-20; Luke 4:18,19; John 17:14-18; Acts 1:4; 2:1,5,39; 17:6; Ephesians 6:12; 2 Timothy 1:7

OVERVIEW

Just how practical is this mandate to bless every nation or people group? It seems as if there's just too much to be done in reviving the Church, in evangelizing our cultures that have churches and in establishing churches in every remaining unreached people.

The task of The Great Commission is so huge that most believers see it only as an ideal. But by following God's basic principles illustrated in the early church, we can join with the zealots of a hundred years ago and say realistically, "It can be done. It must be done. It shall be done."

AIMS

By the end of this small group session, participants will:

- Acknowledge the practicality of the task of discipling the nations when we move according to God's principles;
- Feel encouraged about where we are in God's program;
- Commit to acting on at least one of those basic principles.

LESSON COMMENTARY

INTRODUCTION

It's one thing to see believers encouraged that God is on His throne, that Jesus Christ is really building His Church and the gates of hell aren't standing against it. It's another thing to get very practical and ask, "Just how is this 'making disciples of every *ethne*' supposed to happen?"

Especially if in your small group session you have participants who were not part of the *A Sunday for the World* activities, doing the job of world evangelization will be a very vague, idealistic concept.

"UN-DISCIPLED"?

People groups that don't have an indigenous, viable church movement have had various labels. You might have heard them called "hidden peoples," "unreached peoples," "adoptable peoples," "least-reached" or "least-evangelized peoples." Technically, each of these terms has a distinct definition. But generally, these phrases refer to a people without a strong church. Remember this doesn't refer to individuals but to whole cultures.

For example, in an "unreached people" there may be some true believers in Christ. Also, in a "reached" people such as the Anglo-American people group, although there is a strong, indigenous church movement, there are still millions of unsaved *individuals*.

Don't confuse your study group with this sort of rhetoric at this point. Simply encourage them to begin thinking of the world as the Bible frames it—not as political countries but as people groups. Some have a strong church and some don't.

The Global Plan

"The Great Commission" and "world evangelization" are grandiose terms. But neither, actually, is biblical.

What God does talk about in Scripture is "blessing the nations" (Genesis 12:1-3; Psalm 67:1,2 and other passages glimpsed in the Adult Bible Lesson in *A Sunday for the World*) and "discipling the nations" (Matthew 28:18-20). *Nations*, as discussed in *A Sunday for the World* material, is biblically understood as "ethnic groups, people groups or peoples"—rather than as *countries* in our usual usage. There are a set number of people groups that have not been "discipled."

Historians guess there may have been as many as 60,000 tiny *ethne* or people groups at the time of Christ. That's a lot of discipling to be done.

In the ensuing years, many of those tiny people groups have merged through commerce, language acquisition, migration to cities, etc. Today, depending on definitions of a people, there may be about 12,000 people group clusters on the face of the earth.

The elite of Christian researchers worldwide agree that the people groups not yet approached at all with the Good News number only about 600. With these never-approached included, the number of those peoples where a strong church movement has not occurred is about 2,000.

(These 2,000 are technically clusters that comprise smaller distinct groups/clans/dialects that could number a total of 10,000. This 10,000 number is a guesstimate. That is, as one of the 2,000 are blessed with a solid, indigenous church movement, the Good News might not naturally spread. We might find that what we thought was one people is actually three or four distinct peoples. Thus researchers guess that possibly 10,000 "un-discipled" *ethne* are actually out there within the 2,000 clusters. But don't bore or confuse your small group with these details; see box.)

We have the names and locations, the languages and populations of each of these 2,000. For now, the Harvest Field is very specific.

Meanwhile, the Harvest Force is also specific. The number of committed, true believers in Jesus Christ is currently about 560,000,000—10 percent of world population. If, for discussion's sake, they were divided into congregations of 80 (the average size of the average church worldwide), there would be seven million congregations of committed believers worldwide.

The ratio of the Harvest Force congregations to the Harvest Field un-discipled peoples is something your small group will enjoy calculating. (See Lesson Plan.)

Yet most believers still feel that world evangelization is, in reality, impossible. Why?

Tainted Worldview

When world news is always bad, when we rarely hear about God's global victories, when missionaries are always too few and too under-capitalized, discipling the nations simply seems too big to handle.

With that in mind, many Christians simply focus on the arena they believe they can do something about: their own lives. When that arena proves immensely difficult ("I lost my job"; "I can't keep the kids

out of that mud hole!"; "I'm flunking art!"), even pretending we can be like the early Christians and "turn the world upside down" (see Acts 17:6) seems very unrealistic.

Marketers tell us the average North American is barraged with 2,000 "messages" per day. And most of them are negative: *You're not good enough without our product. The world is going to the dogs. Everyone lives in sin. You need to....* In desperation, many Christians throw their arms around their family with, "I can't change the world. But I can make a difference right here in my own house. I'll protect my family against the encroachment of evil from all sides. And I'll hope Jesus comes back soon."

But is defensiveness a biblical posture? Are we urging fellow believers to be afraid of the world? God has not given us the spirit of fear but of power, love and of a sound mind (see 2 Timothy 1:7).

Defensiveness, fear of the world's evil and escapist dreams about the Rapture aren't exactly the biblical disciple's ways of viewing the world.

A Biblical Worldview

The Bible constantly reminds us that we are flesh and spirit, body and soul. And as such we have a foot in both "worlds"—the world of Satan's evil system as well as the physical, tangible world of humanity. (Actually, the word *world* [Greek *kosmos*] as it is used in the New Testament carries perhaps seven different meanings. It makes a great word study.) We are to be in the (natural, tangible) world but not of the (Satanic, spiritual) world system (see John 17:14-18).

In the spiritual dimension, our response to the world is to take a stand and fight—being very careful about who our enemy is:

> "For our struggle is not against flesh and blood,
> but against the rulers, against the powers, against
> the world forces of this darkness, against the
> spiritual forces of wickedness in the heavenly
> places" (Ephesians 6:12).

In the natural dimension, our response to the human world is to serve. We can fulfill needs, and we can share the gospel of salvation in Jesus Christ with all those who are enslaved captives of the evil world system. We are to:

> "Preach the gospel to the poor, ...to proclaim
> release to the captives, and recovery of sight to
> the blind, to set free those who are downtrodden,
> to proclaim the favorable year of the Lord"
> (Luke 4:18,19; see also Isaiah 61:1).

Small Group Study

Christianity in this world isn't about our having a good life and praying fervently that things will go well for us. That's called heaven. Christianity is being infused with the presence of Jesus Christ to fight the good fight and rescue the perishing.

Principled Activists

If we ever get roused about impacting the world, we usually think first in terms of actions. What do we *do?*

But before we jump into action to turn the world upside down, we need to be sure we're not running ahead of God, but moving out according to His principles, not our enthusiasm. Four of those basic principles are evident in the passages we'll look at in this session:

- God blesses an obedient church;
- God blesses a unified church;
- God blesses a strategic church;
- God blesses a multiplying church.

All these principles of blessing, of course, point back to the central message of *A Sunday for the World*:

> God blesses us,
>
> That all the ends of the earth may fear Him
>
> (Psalm 67:7).

How can we encourage fellow believers to realistically face the world? By helping them adopt a biblical worldview, one that assertively, confidently seeks to impact the world through ministry that is obedient, unified, strategic and reproducing. When the Body of Christ is moving out according to those principles, the task of world evangelization is very, very do-able. It can be done!

For Further Study

The following are highly recommended general Bible studies for small groups on the global purpose of God.

- *Destination 2000* is a video-based Bible study by international Bible teacher Bob Sjogren. An overview of the biblical basis of God's global enterprise, this sharp video study is particularly designed for small groups and Bible classes. Contact Frontiers, 325 N. Stapley Dr., Mesa, AZ 85203; Phone: 800-607-3783.
- *Catch the Vision 2000* by Bill and Amy Stearns is a book-based Bible study course for individuals and small groups. Stunning stories of God's move worldwide and challenging group Bible studies combine as participants read a chapter of *Catch the Vision 2000* and then work through the group study guide week by week. Available at your local Christian bookstore from Bethany House Publishers or call 800-MISSION.
- *No Turning Back* by George Verwer is a book that couples the essentials of personal discipleship with the scope of God's global purpose. The disciplines of the vibrant Christian life are studied within the context of global discipleship. Available at your local Christian bookstore from O.M. Lit Publishers.

LESSON PLAN

1. Carefully study this session's Bible passages and read through the Lesson Commentary.
2. Thoroughly study the Lesson Plan below. It amplifies many of the points of the Lesson Commentary.
3. Pray that your study group will know, feel and act on the objectives for the session.
4. Prepare materials and equipment as listed below.

MATERIALS NEEDED

- Bibles;
- Photocopies of Student Worksheets;
- A white board, chalkboard or flipchart and appropriate felt-tip pens.

SESSION AT A GLANCE

Follow the normal schedule of your small group sessions. Simply insert the following interactive Bible study. If this is not a regular program in your fellowship, perhaps divide an hour into:

Fellowship Time, Introductions, Discussion About *A Sunday for the World* Activities (10 Minutes)

The "It Can Be Done" Bible Study (30 Minutes)

Prayer Time (10-20 Minutes or More!)

Refreshments at Close

THE SESSION

BEFORE THE SESSION

Ask an early arriver to draw the harvest chart from the Student Worksheet on the chalkboard. Ask participants in *A Sunday for the World* their opinion of the activities of the day.

Take an informal poll: Do you think the Great Commission can be done? Why or why not?

FELLOWSHIP TIME (10 MINUTES)

STUDY (30 MINUTES)

Introduce the study by initiating the poll question above or summarizing your findings from earlier polling.

Say **Do most believers think the Great Commission can be *done?* Finished?** Most of the "why not" responses from Christians come from our mindset that says the world is a huge, teeming mass of hurting individuals. And there are more all the time. Some believers feel that going everywhere and telling everyone the

Small Group Study

gospel isn't actually realistic; it's just a nice ideal.

But let's see how realistic God's global plan is. We get a clear glimpse from the early church's first Day of Pentecost.

Instruct participants to follow the chart on their Student Worksheets and to turn to Acts 1.

Year	Harvest Force	Harvest Field	Ratio	Methods	Principles
A.D. 35:					
Today:					

Ask your group the following questions and fill in answers as you work your way across the chart. Lightly remind participants not to get too theologically picky about each question. (For example, it could be argued that the Church's first Day of Pentecost was possibly not in A.D. 35, the upper room disciples were technically not yet a "congregation," etc.)

Let's turn to the first couple of chapters of Acts—on the morning of the Acts Day of Pentecost A.D. 35.

The Harvest Force

Let's look at the harvest force. How many congregations of believers were there? (One.) How many believers in that congregation? (120.)

The Harvest Field

Let's look at the harvest field. How many *ethne* or nations were there? (Missiologists guess about 60,000! These were usually very small tribal groups.) How many of those nations had a Christian presence—a strong enough church to eventually evangelize its own people? (One—the Jewish people.) So—possibly—how many unreached peoples were there at this time? (Possibly 59,999!) So what's the ratio of congregations per unreached people? (One congregation to 59,999 nations to disciple!)

Methods

Let's look at the methods—on a practical, human level—which were available to these early disciples. How could the disciples travel to disciple all those 59,999 nations? (Drawing these items on the chalkboard under the "Methodology" usually brings some humor into the presentation. Most will suggest travel by foot, horse or donkey, ox cart, chariot, ship or camel.) Once they arrived, how could they proclaim the gospel? (Virtually all suggestions boil down to the fact that—after drama, living their faith, signs and wonders, etc.—the gospel had to be explained orally or in written form.)

Principles

With just five or six travel methods and just two methods of proclamation, these disciples turned the world upside down. How? This overwhelming task for the 120 disciples in the Upper Room would be very do-able as long as the Church followed God's global principles. Let's look carefully at each reference:

• Acts 1:4

What He said, they did. Although there were thousands who followed Jesus around, there were only 120 who specifically did what He said, and these are the ones on whom God's power fell. The principle is:

God uses an obedient church.

• Acts 2:1

They were all together in one place. Jesus prayed for us believers, that we all would be one as He and the Father are one—that the world may believe that He is sent from God (see John 17:21). Every believer is different, just as the parts of the body are different. Every group of true believers is different, with differing traditions, styles of worship and personalities. But all true believers can work together even while maintaining our own identities, convictions and traditions. The principle is:

God uses a unified church.

• Acts 2:5

Rather than sending 120 out to 59,999 people groups by donkey, ox cart or on foot, God strategically brought representatives of the nations to Jerusalem for that historic Day of Pentecost. There were some representatives from every people group "under heaven." Israel was the commercial crossroads of the inhabited world at that time. God may have prompted a trader years before to head for Jerusalem from the shores of China, may have orchestrated the marriage of a foreigner and a Jew to live in Jerusalem. Is God big enough to strategically place individuals for the furtherance of His great purpose? Of course. Rather than attempting lots of *good* things for the Kingdom, the disciples could simply fall into what God was already doing—the *best, most strategic* things—and then move with Him. The principle is to move in God's strategies, because:

God uses a strategic church.

• Acts 2:39

After new disciples were first *added,* they began *multiplying.* The message, just as the message of this lesson we're studying right now, was not just for them. It was for them and their families. But further, it was for them, their families and for all those who were afar off. The Good News is to be multiplied. Ministry that impacts people is never an end in itself. Those impacted are to be trained to go and do likewise. The principle is:

God uses a multiplying church.

NOW, AS OF TODAY

The Harvest Force

How many congregations are there today? Let's not consider nominal Christians, since we can't count on them, right? If we grouped only the committed believers into congregations of about 80 each—the average size of churches around the world—how many churches of committed believers would we have? (After guesses, suggest an estimated 7 million. Be prepared for questions later, since many dedicated researchers worldwide disagree on this figure—depending on one's definition of a "committed believer"—of the average size of a church, etc.) **An educated guess would be perhaps 7,000,000 congregations. And how many committed believers are in those 7 million churches?** (From the *A Sunday for the World* demonstration, coach your small group to figure 10 percent of today's world population—which is about 5.6 billion. Here again, researchers have varying numbers.) **Perhaps there are 560 million committed believers.**

The Harvest Field

How many people groups remain to be discipled? (Note: Don't bother with the background discussions about exactly how many remaining unreached peoples there are. There may be 10,000; there may be clusters of only 2,000. Our purpose here isn't training missiologists or statisticians.) **There are perhaps about 2,000 people groups. What is the ratio today of congregations per unreached people group?** (Remind participants that the A.D. 35 ratio was one congregation for maybe 59,999 people groups. For today's ratio, let participants guess or pull out their calculators. The more they have to interact with the information, the more impact it will have.) **Perhaps 3,500 congregations of committed believers for every one remaining unreached people.**

What might happen if 3,500 congregations of committed believers focused their prayers on one unreached people? What if they took up just one offering, polled their members for those who would go as a pre-evangelism team or a church-planting team? How many incredible resources could be concentrated on that one unreached people?

Methods

Now, what advantages does today's massive harvest force have in methods? Think of transportation: We can be anywhere in the world within 24 hours. And what about methods of proclaiming the gospel today? (If time permits, allow the group to brainstorm methods of proclamation—video, radio, audiocassettes, mass printing, etc.)

Principles

God's principles are the same today as ever. Let's face it—if the Church will act in obedience, in unity, according to God's strategies and with a view toward multiplication, the remaining task is wonderfully do-able.

CONCLUSION

Let your group respond in discussion to **Well, what do you think?**

Somewhere in the discussion be sure to insert the concept that what God is doing in the big picture is specific and realistic. So how He uses us in that plan is specific and realistic.

Encourage your group that this doesn't have to be the end of the study or discussion on the big picture of what God is doing. Refer to the recommended resources to help shape our understanding of our place in God's great global plan.

PRAYER TIME (10-20 MINUTES OR MORE!)

REFRESHMENTS AT CLOSE

STUDENT WORKSHEET

PRINCIPLES IN GOD'S GLOBAL PLAN

Fill in the chart as you study and discuss:

Year	Harvest Force	Harvest Field	Ratio	Methods	Principles
		A.D. 35: Acts 1:4			
		Acts 2:1			
		Acts 2:5			
		Acts 2:39			
Today:					

RESOURCES FOR FURTHER STUDY AND INFORMATION

Studies

Destination 2000 is a video Bible study based on the book *Unveiled at Last* by Bob Sjogren. An overview of the biblical basis of God's global enterprise, this sharp video study is particularly designed for small groups

Catch the Vision 2000 by Bill and Amy Stearns is a book-based Bible study course for individuals and small groups. It features stunning stories of God's move worldwide and challenging group Bible studies.

No Turning Back by George Verwer is a book that couples the essentials of personal discipleship with the scope of God's global purpose. Available at your local Christian bookstore from O.M. Lit Publishers.

Ask for any of the above at your Christian bookstore or call 800-MISSION.

Genesys Computer Network

Want to get in on all the updates of what God is doing in the worldwide Body of Christ today? Get a free session on the Christian computer network called Genesys for yourself or a friend with a computer and modem. You'll get a glimpse into this worldwide network of information, breakthroughs, prayer news, training and global contacts. Phone 703-750-0318 for a complimentary session; or Fax: 703-642-3841; or Internet: sysop@gen.org.

FOLLOW-UP ACTION STEPS

WHAT'S AFTER A SUNDAY FOR THE WORLD?

What do you do after *A Sunday for the World*? First, you relax for a few days. Next, you consider your personal role as a mobilizer—a discipler with a global perspective—and work through the mobilizer training video-seminar called *Make a Difference* (see Resources). This will help equip you to build mission vision momentum throughout your church. Some of the suggestions in the *Make a Difference* training include the following four key steps:

STEP 1: GET THEM INTO THE WORD

Immediately get your fellowship back into the Bible to catch a global perspective of what God has been saying all along. Offer one of the following solid Bible study courses to as many classes as possible at the same time. (Order from your Christian bookstore or toll-free by phoning 800-MISSION. See Resources for additional study materials.)

Study either:

- *Catch the Vision 2000* by Bill and Amy Stearns (Bethany House Publishers)

Catch the Vision 2000 is a book-based Bible study on the biblical, historical, cultural and strategic aspects of finding your part in God's global plan. Each participant reads a chapter of the award-winning *Catch the Vision 2000* text, and a Leader's Guide has reproducible worksheets for participants in weekly Bible study. The 12- or 13-session course is formatted to fit your current Bible study schedule, and is adaptable for high school study sessions.

Or:

- *Destination 2000* by Bob Sjogren (Frontiers)

Destination 2000 is a fast-paced video series of solid Bible studies on the theme of God's heart for every people. A group leader's guide accompanies each half-hour of video teaching by international Bible teacher Bob Sjogren of Frontiers. Twelve sessions match a quarter of Sunday School, home group or other Bible study formats for adults. Covering much of the same Bible material as *Catch the Vision 2000*, *Destination 2000's* video format is extremely simple to present and ensures a certain quality control of the teaching.

- *The Great KidMission*

This resource is a compendium of ideas and resources for involving children in active learning about missions around the world. The book contains a great variety of resources to meet the needs of those who want to create a customized five- to ten-day Children's Missions Conference, extend Vacation Bible School or enrich Kids' Club and Sunday School programs.

- *Destination 2000 for Kids!* by Bob Sjogren and Jill Harris (Frontiers)

All the solid Bible lessons presented in the above adult curricula are reflected in this study program for children. With varying learning activities for each age group up through juniors, *Destination 2000 for Kids!* will introduce your children to key biblical concepts on God's heart for the world, and will give you information on further cutting-edge mission resources for children.

See Resources for other materials you might review.

STEP 2: LINK UP TO GET ONGOING INFORMATION

Get up-to-the-minute reports of what God is doing globally, of new resources and worldwide prayer needs by subscribing to a free e-mail service called Brigada. This solidly evangelical network supplies key updates and directs you to dozens of other sources of mission input. Find someone in your group who is currently using e-mail through any server such as CompuServe, America-On-Line, Prodigy, etc. Ask that person—perhaps a junior high student!—to send a message to: hub@xc.org. The subject area is to be left blank—perhaps by hitting the space bar.

The message is simple: Subscribe Brigada. Brigada will link your fellowship up to what's happening in the rest of the Body of Christ.

Browse through a virtual library/bookstore of everything you'll need to move your fellowship on in a vision of God's heart for all peoples through the Global Exchange Network—Genesys. Genesys can clue your church in on what the rest of the Body of Christ is doing worldwide. It's an on-line computer network owned and operated by a solidly Christian nonprofit ministry.

Find someone in your group who has a computer and modem, and both of you can enjoy a free session on Genesys. This global information source is available in most locations through a local call via MCI and British Telecom. It carries more breakthrough news, global prayer requests, opportunities for short- and long-term ministry, files on countries and people groups, lists and reviews of the world's best mission materials and resources, prayer training lessons, articles and how-to manuals on going, welcoming, sending and mobilizing and more. It also gives you e-mail capabilities to other believers across the planet as well as to use as your everyday e-mail service. There is a monthly service fee comparable to the commercial on-line services. To sign on for a free session, contact Global Exchange Network, 3686 King St., Suite 182, Alexandria, VA 22302; Phone: 703-750-0318, Fax: 703-642-3841; E-mail: sysop@gen.org.

STEP 3: ENCOURAGE OTHER CONGREGATIONS TO NEW VISION

You can help mobilize other fellowships to a vision of God's heart for every people.

- Encourage them to host *A Sunday for the World*.
- Pass along the above information on how they can try out Genesys.

- Consider approaching other fellowships in your community to host a joint "Concert of Prayer." This is a community-wide gathering to pray for your churches, your community, your country and the world. For information and a training program for hosting Concerts of Prayer, contact: Concerts of Prayer International; Phone: 708-690-8441, Fax: 708-690-0160.

- Take a media person to lunch. Local Christian media are always on the lookout for good news. And vision-building news in the newspapers and on your local radio and television stations can encourage your entire community of churches. For example: Take a newspaper religion editor to lunch. Often these editors only get the world's bad news or the dry, institutional news from religious organizations. Forward to her or him the breakthrough anecdotes, stories and statistics you get from your ongoing connections (as suggested above) with the worldwide Body of Christ.

STEP 4: KEEP GETTING EXPERT INPUT

As a fellowship, make good use of your denomination's or association's mission departments. In addition, join one of the following general organizations that will serve your needs for mission expertise and information:

- ACMC is Advancing Churches in Mission Commitment. Contact them at: ACMC, P.O. Box ACMC, Wheaton, IL 60187; Phone: 800-798-2262.

- AIMS—the Association of International Mission Services—is for charismatically oriented fellowships. Contact them at: AIMS, P.O. Box 64534, Virginia Beach, VA 23464; Phone: 804-579-5850.

RESOURCES

The following are only a few of the hundreds of wonderful resources available on God's heart for every people. Be sure to connect with the mission office of your denomination or affiliation of churches, to ask for resource catalogs from your favorite mission agencies and to connect with these suppliers of key materials.

PRAYER RESOURCES

Operation World, by Patrick Johnstone (Zondervan Publishers); To order call 800-MISSION or request it at your local Christian bookstore. Statistics and prayer information on every country in the world.

You Can Change the World, by Jill Johnstone (Zondervan Publishers); To order call 800-MISSION or request it at your local Christian bookstore. This is "Operation World" for elementary age children. Very colorful and informative.

Global Prayer Digest; U. S. Center for World Mission, 1605 Elizabeth St., Pasadena, CA 91104; Phone: 818-797-1111. A daily guide for prayer for unreached nations and peoples. Published monthly.

ADULT EDUCATION

All materials listed below can be requested at your local Christian bookstore or ordered from William Carey Library (1-800-MISSION) or the publishers listed.

Destination 2000, Frontiers, 325 N. Stapley Dr., Mesa, AZ 85203; Phone: 800-60-SERVE (800-607-3783). (See Follow-up Action Steps.) Twelve-part Bible study video course with discussion guide. Excellent, solid and fast-paced program that surprises many mature believers with its impact and insights drawn from many familiar passages throughout the Bible.

Catch the Vision 2000, by Bill and Amy Stearns (Bethany House Publishers) and Study Guide (World Christian Inc.). (See Follow-up Action Steps.) A user-friendly Sunday School class or home group Bible study on God's global plan and our part in it.

Serving as Senders, by Neal Pirolo; Emmaus Road International, 7150 Tanner Court, San Diego, CA 92111. A group discussion and guide to help believers on the home front get serious about backing up their team on the field with communication expertise, prayer mobilization, fund raising, research, etc.

Working Your Way to the Nations, Jon Lewis, editor; contact William Carey Library; Phone: 800-MISSION. A practical guide to help tentmakers prepare to penetrate restricted access nations.

Perspectives on the World Christian Movement; Perspectives Study Program, 1605 Elizabeth St., Pasadena, CA 91104; Phone: 818-398-2125. A 16-week, intensive, life-changing course on the biblical basis and history of missions, culture and strategic factors in world evangelization, etc. Can be taken via extension courses in dozens of locations in North America, by correspondence or in resident courses. There is also a book by the same title available through the William Carey Library, 1-800-MISSION.

CHILDREN'S RESOURCES

The Great KidMission; Gospel Light Publications, 2300 Knoll Dr., Ventura, CA 93003; Phone: 800-446-7735; Fax: 800-860-3109. This resource is a compendium of ideas and resources for involving children in active learning about missions around the world. The book contains a great variety of resources to meet the needs of those who want to create a customized five- to ten-day Children's Missions Conference, extend Vacation Bible School or enrich Kids' Club and Sunday School programs.

Missions Curriculum for Children; Crossroads Publications, P.O. Box 11475, Campbell, CA 95011; Phone: 408-378-6658; Fax: 408-241-2545. Affordable curricula available that focus on China, Pakistan, Romania and other countries. Children love it. Good for Sunday Schools or VBS.

KidsCan Network Catalog; Jan Bell, Kids Can Make a Difference, 4445 Webster Dr., York, PA 17402; Phone: 800-543-7554, Fax: 717-757-6103, Internet: kidscan@xc.org. A resource center for children's world-Christian curricula and materials. Quality, solidly biblical children's mission materials.

M and M Kids; Jill Harris, Frontiers, 325 N. Stapley Dr., Mesa, AZ 85203; Phone: 800-60-SERVE (800-607-3783). Teacher training as well as missions conference for children. This is highly recommended.

Destination 2000 for Kids!; Bob Sjogren and Jill Harris, Frontiers, 325 N. Stapley Dr., Mesa, AZ 85203; Phone: 800-60-SERVE (800-607-3783). A Bible study curriculum for children with varying learning activities for each age group up through sixth grade.

Children's Mission Resource Center; Gerry Dueck, U.S. Center for World Mission, 1605 Elizabeth St., Pasadena, CA 91104; Phone: 818-797-1111. A library of resources available for teaching children about missions.

Mini Mission Conference for Children by Dorothy Holsinger Schultz; R.C. Law & Co., Inc., 4861 Chino Ave., Chino, CA 91710; Phone: 800-777-5292. Seven-part course for Sunday School, VBS or missions conference.

Kids Pray; Tim and Julie Brown, 3910 E. El Paso Drive, Flagstaff, AZ 86004-2336; Phone: 520-526-0875. These materials provide creative ways to teach children to pray effectively for the world.

Kids Cruise the Globe; John and Eldora Schwab, 3465 Fosberg Rd., Turlock, CA 95382; Phone: 209-668-8734. Missions curriculum for children for four Sundays. Covers what missions is like in different areas of the world—complete with videos for each week.

Is This Missions Thing for Real? by Bob Putman; ACMC (Advancing Churches in Missions Commitment), P.O. Box ACMC, Wheaton, IL 60189; Phone: 800-798-2262. Upbeat, humorous and on target with high-schoolers, this 13-week curriculum seeks to dispel common missionary stereotypes and to educate about contemporary missions.

VIDEOS AND CASSETTES

10/40 Window Video for Children and *Prayerwalking for Kids* (*How to Pray for Your City*); Joey and Fawn Parish, 6673 Sora Street, Ventura, CA 93003; Phone: 805-650-3511. These are fast-paced, wonderful videos to orient children to the idea of praying for the 10/40 Window.

Caleb Project Videos for Children; Caleb Project, 10 West Dry Creek Circle, Littleton, CO 80120-4170; Phone: 303-730-4170; Fax: 303-730-4177; Internet: Info@cproject.com. Two videos for children are available: Patna, India and Urban Malays.

Countdown 2000 Video Series; U.S. Center for World Mission, 1605 E. Elizabeth St., Pasadena, CA 91104. Phone: 800-MISSION. A series of clear, you-are-there videos about how God is breaking through to various unreached people groups. The first two have three segments each—ideal for small group viewing.

Ee Taow!; New Tribes Mission, Destination Summit Media, 1000 E. First St., Sanford, FL 32771-1487; Phone: 407-323-3430. (30 min.) This intriguing, uplifting story is a textbook look at how God can use anyone to "let the peoples be glad." The second half is simply an infomercial for Summit ministries, but the first half is dynamite regardless of your mission agency affiliation.

Doing Your Bit; True Colours Productions. Distributed in the U.S. by the U.S. Center for World Mission, 1605 E. Elizabeth St., Pasadena, CA 91104; Phone: 800-MISSION. (10 min.) Probably worldwide the best there is for a brief overview of people-group thinking and the adopt-a-people strategy. Entertaining and clearly educational for youth and adults.

The Wait of the World; Gospel Films, P.O. Box 455, Muskegon, MI 49443; Phone: 616-773-3361. (90 min.) A classic mission film—not necessarily missiologically on the cutting edge, but a good, thought-provoking story for youth and adults.

NETWORKING AGENCIES

ACMC, P.O. Box ACMC, Wheaton, IL 60189; Phone: 800-798-2262. Helping churches mobilize through training, resources and consultation.

AIMS, P.O. Box 64534 Virginia Beach, VA 23464; Phone: 804-579-5850. Provides conferences and resources for mobilizing churches, especially in the renewal movement.

A.D. 2000 and Beyond; 2860 S. Circle Dr., Suite 2112, Colorado Springs, CO 80906; Phone: 719-576-2000. A loose network of organizations working in their various geographic and interest areas.

The Antioch Network, 7854 Nichols, Lemon Grove, CA 91945. Helps link churches which are directly active in sending their own mission teams.

Intercristo, 19303 Fremont Ave. North, Seattle, WA 98133; Phone: 800-426-1342. An interdenominational service agency of evangelical tradition, providing guidance and information to help mission agencies locate qualified personnel.

NEWSLETTERS

World Pulse, P.O. Box 794, Wheaton, IL 60189; Phone: 708-653-2158. A must-read bi-weekly publication of missions news from around the world, upcoming events, plus one article that focuses on a specific region of the world.

National and International Religion Report, P.O. Box 21505, Roanoke, VA 24018; Phone: 703-989-7500. A bi-weekly summary of national and international news. Excellent for busy people.

Mobilizer, P.O. Box ACMC, Wheaton, IL 60189; Phone: 800-798-2262. A quarterly publication which is designed to help the mission task force of a local church be more effective.

MARC Newsletter, 121 E. Huntington Dr., Monrovia, CA 91016; Phone: 818-303-8811. A quarterly letter World Vision publishes focusing on the poor and ways we can bring the Gospel to them in a holistic manner.

MAGAZINES

Among the hundreds of very good mission magazines produced by mission agencies and denominational mission offices, the following are especially helpful in getting your fellowship up to speed:

Evangelical Missions Quarterly, P.O. Box 794, Wheaton, IL 60189; Phone: 708-653-2158. A quarterly publication for field missionaries, missions pastors and
administrators.

Mission Frontiers; U. S. Center for World Mission, 1605 Elizabeth St., Pasadena, CA 91104. Published bi-monthly from the U.S. Center, focuses attention on the
unreached peoples in the world and reports what God is doing through western missionaries.

The Great Commission Handbook, Berry Publishing, 701 Main St., Evanston, IL 60202; Phone: 708-869-1573. Annual publication filled with excellent articles on missions. When ordering, ask for the present year's date.

International Journal of Frontier Mission, P.O. Box 27266, El Paso, TX 79926. A quarterly journal that discusses practical ways to reach the unreached with the gospel.

BOOKS AND MAPS SOURCES

William Carey Library, PO Box 40129, Pasadena CA 91114; For a free catalog call 800-MISSION. For the best selection at the best prices, look no further.

MARC, 121 E. Huntington Dr., Monrovia, CA 91016; Phone: 818-303-8811. Specialized books that address the needs of the unreached, the poor and marginalized people in the world.

Global Mapping, 7899 Lexington Dr., Suite 200A, Colorado Springs, CO 80920; Phone: 719-531-3599. Excellent resources available that map out the advances of the church and strongholds of the enemy.

Resources

MISSIONS TASK FORCE RESOURCES

Make a Difference: Moblizing Your Church to New Mission Vision!; Produced by ProclaMedia and World Christian Inc. Order from ProclaMedia, P.O. Box 26479, Colorado Springs, CO 80936; Phone: 719-380-0505. Features several key "generic" mobilization organizations. This four-hour video-based training seminar equips mission mobilizers to serve their fellowships as they move toward more strategic global involvement. Trains you how to help your group catch a vision, build that vision and finally strategically act out their vision of God's global plan. Perfect for missions task force training, crucial for individual mobilizers.

ACMC Church Membership; ACMC, P.O. Box ACMC, Wheaton, IL 60189; Phone: 800-798-2262. Your fellowship can join the "generic" mission network called Advancing Churches in Mission Commitment. Membership opens your church to conferences, consultation and key materials such as the ACMC *Missions Policy Handbook and Missions Conference Planner.* Even if you don't join as a church, be sure to request a full listing of ACMC's resources.

AIMS Church Membership; AIMS, P.O. Box 64534, Virginia Beach, VA 23464; Phone: 804-579-5850. Especially if your church is active in the renewal movement, the Association of International Mission Services can provide you with studies, seminars, resources, conferences, a directory and outreach opportunities worldwide. Request a list of AIMS services and materials.

Faith Promise, by Norm Lewis; Phone: 800-MISSION to order. Great book in a straightforward style that communicates with ordinary pew-sitters about the value of the faith-promise method of mission support.

SHORT TERM TEAM RESOURCES

Launching the Great Go-Mission, by Lincoln Murdoch; Step Up to Life Press, Omaha, NE; Phone: 402-330-5724 to order. Short term team training book and resource guide on a local church level.

Vacation with a Purpose, by Eaton and Hurst; Available through your local Christian bookstore or 800-MISSION. Handbook for short-term missions experience. Leader's guide and workbook available.

Stepping Out, by Steve Hawthorne, Editor; Berry Publishing Services, 701 Main, Evanston, IL 60202, Phone: 708-869-1573. Guide to short-term missions, with dozens of articles on topics crucial to short-term experiences.

SEMINARS

Destination 2000; Contact Bob Sjogren, Frontiers, 625 N. Stapley Dr., Mesa, AZ 85203; Phone: 800-60-SERVE (800-607-3783). Excellent, solid and fast-paced program that surprises many mature believers with its impact and insights drawn from many familiar passages throughout the Bible. A tremendous introduction to the unifying theme in Scripture of God's heart for all peoples.

Catch the Vision 2000; Bill and Amy Stearns, World Christian Inc., Box 1010, Colorado Springs CO 80901; Phone: 719-635-4567, Internet: world.christian@gen.org. Bill and Amy Stearns present an entertaining, creative seminar designed for those with virtually no or low

Resources

interest in what God is doing globally. Solid Bible study, encouraging global reports, refreshing approaches to the very do-able challenge of bringing the Gospel to every people, tribe, tongue and nation.

Run With the Vision; Bill and Amy Stearns, World Christian Inc., Box 1010, Colorado Springs CO 80901; Phone: 719-635-4567, Internet: world.christian@gen.org. *Run With the Vision* is a basic training course for mission mobilizers. It presumes participants are up-to-speed on what God is doing globally and on elemental missiological concepts. Equips those with a heart to serve the church with principles and tools to move whole churches to a vision beyond themselves.

7 Dynamics; Larry Walker, ACMC Southwest Regional Director; Phone: 619-746-4285. A practical seminar that will help move missions forward in your church. Extremely helpful nuts and bolts of "doing missions" and organizing properly for it in the local church. Learn how to communicate missions in a contemporary manner.

Partnering with the Church in the Developing World; Kevin Guttman, Partners International Area Representative; P.O. Box 15025, San Jose, CA 95115; Phone: 800-966-5515. Seminar is 30 minutes and utilizes colorful overheads and an outline on the agonies and ecstasies of churches in global partnerships—with indigenous ministries of the Two-Thirds World, with other cultures' churches and with mission agencies.

BULLETIN INSERTS

Church Around the World; Tyndale House, 351 Executive Dr., Carol Stream, IL 60188, Phone: 708-668-8300. A monthly two-sided insert with highlights of what God is doing around the world where the Church is already planted.

FrontierSCAN; U. S. Center for World Mission, 1605 Elizabeth St., Pasadena, CA 91104; Phone: 818-797-1111. A monthly double-sided insert focusing on the unreached/frontier people groups that the gospel has yet to penetrate.

The Final Frontiers; AIMS, P.O. Box 64534, Virginia Beach, VA 23464; Phone: 804-579-5850. A monthly double-sided insert that focuses on specific countries or unreached people groups.

INFORMATION

Christian Information Network; CIN, 11025 Hwy 83, Colorado Springs, CO 80921; Phone: 719-522-1040; Internet: CompuServe 73422,3471. Supplies vital information to over 28,000 churches worldwide regarding the 10/40 Window and the Prayer Through the Window emphases.

Brigada; Internet: hub@xc.org. An on-line network of missions-minded people who want to network together to complete the Great Commission. To participate send a message to hub@xc.org and in the message area (leave subject blank) type: *subscribe Brigada*

Global Glimpses; Internet: jhanna@cproject.com. Caleb Project weekly releases three or four breakthroughs in the global harvest. To receive these in your e-mail box, send a request to Internet address.

Genesys; 3686 King St., Suite 182, Alexandria, VA 22302; Phone: 703-750-0318; Fax: 703-642-3841; Internet: sysop@gen.org. This

Resources

computer network of the Christian nonprofit Global Exchange Network is an ongoing resource that can keep you updated on all of the best materials, opportunities, breakthroughs, background files, global prayer alerts and more—as well as allow e-mail with world Christians across the planet. Phone, e-mail or write for a free sample session.

People Group Consultant; Internet: hub@xc.org. This database on the world's unreached peoples is accessible with a simple request. Send a message to hub@xc.org that states: Search _____ (Fill in the name of the people group you're researching.). A batch of information on that people automatically comes back to your e-mail box.

DRAMA/SKITS

A View from on High and 15 other scripts; Caleb Project, 10 West Dry Creek Circle, Littleton, CO 80010; Phone: 303-730-4170. Two angels discuss missions and people in a humorous way.

Yardwork and *A Missions Carol*; ACMC, P.O. Box ACMC, Wheaton, IL 60189; Phone: 800-798-2262. Both show God's heart for the world through drama.

Who Will Fill Our Shoes?; New Hope, P.O. Box 12065, Birmingham, AL 35202-2065; Phone: 205-991-4933. A collection of 13 dramatic sketches for missions awareness.

Gospel Enterprise; Kevin Guttman, 11571 College Ave., Garden Grove, CA 92640; Phone: 714-530-1375. Star Trek-based theme to explain trends in missions.

200